Pools of Lodging for the Moon

Pools of Lodging

DAVID K. REYNOLDS,
PH.D.

for the Moon

Strategy for
a Positive Life-Style

WILLIAM MORROW AND COMPANY, INC.
NEW YORK

Grateful acknowledgment is made for permission to excerpt portions of the Japanese Moritist magazine *Seikatsu no Hakken*.

Library of Congress Cataloging-in-Publication Data

Reynolds, David K.
  Pools of lodging for the moon.

  Bibliography: p.
  1. Morita psychotherapy. I. Title.
RC489.M65R52 1989   616.89'14   88–18557
ISBN 0-688-08156-8

Printed in the United States of America

    2 3 4 5 6 7 8 9 10

BOOK DESIGN BY MARIA EPES

For Lynn
Once Again
Certainly

Acknowledgments

Perhaps I do nothing as well as appreciate what others do better than I. They keep teaching me; so it is my responsibility to write some of the lessons they offer. In truth, I do not write so much as I am written.

A list of my teachers must include Barbara Bogart, Chuck Gallagher, Harold V. Hall, Robert Hillman, Divina Himaya, Milton Winkler, U. Carlisle Hunsaker, Dr. F. Ishu Ishiyama, Kathleen R. Johnson, Dr. A. Kumasaka, Michio Kusama, Susan LaGrande, Elizabeth M. McNeill, Gregoria Marrero, Radmila Moacanin, Brian Ogawa, Alexandra Rejzer, Brad Robinson, Daniel Rybold, Bob Vahle, Priscilla S. Whiteford, Elizabeth Yuin Hamilton, Larry Loomis, Patricia Ryan, Gregg Krech, Said Zadeh, and my wife, Lynn Sanae Reynolds.

In Japan my teachers include Yozo Hasegawa, Hiromu Shimbo, Kenshiro Ohara, Takeo Doi, the late Hiroshi Iwai, Akihisa Kondo, Takehisa Kora, Naotake Shinfuku, Tomonori Suzuki, Ishin Yoshimoto, Akira Ishii, Shue Usami, Mali Kikuchi, Steve Yamamoto, Hatsuko Chiba, Masayo Ohno, and Reiko Omaki.

I appreciate their teachings.

Contents

The water doesn't think of giving it lodging
Nor the moon of lodging there
How clear the reflection!

Songs of the Way of the Spear
in *Zen and the Ways,*
by Trevor Leggett.
New York: Random House, 1987, p. 167.

In the Buddhist teachings the symbol for compassion . . . is one moon shining in the sky while its image is reflected in one hundred bowls of water. The moon does not demand, "If you open to me, I will do you a favor and shine on you." The moon just shines.

Cutting Through Spiritual Materialism
by Trungpa Chogyam.
Berkeley, Calif.: Shambala, 1973, p. 213.

Introduction

For a long time Americans didn't bother to listen to the Japanese. That was a mistake. Many Americans seemed to consider the Japanese to be a strange people with odd customs and nothing of value to offer the West except, perhaps, an exotic religion (Zen), colorful woodblock prints, and, eventually, electrical appliances and automobiles.

I repeat, failing to listen was a mistake. Believing everything we hear or trying to practice everything we hear would be a mistake, also. But listen we must.

The successful comeback of the Japanese after World War II indicates that they have something worth investigating. More importantly, however, we cannot afford to become a people who, because of our pride and success, choose to ignore the lessons that can be learned from others. It can be argued that much of Japan's current international success stems from their very willingness (even eagerness) to learn from others. This openness to learning from other nations is the first lesson we must fully absorb.

Constructive Living offers lessons worthy of our attention. It is based on fundamental principles of human living sketched out by a Japanese professor of psychiatry named Morita and a lay priest named Yoshimoto. These two wrote the basic life recipes you will find in the following pages. I have merely added flavoring to make the taste more palatable for Westerners. Their understandings have been reinterpreted somewhat and elaborated for Westerners here. Try on these ideas; see how well they fit your life. The pattern can be adapted to a variety of people-sizes and ages and colors.

The strategy for positive living in this book may not turn you into an extraordinary person. But it could help you keep from bumping into yourself as you go about achieving your natural potential. Too often we interfere with our own progress. We hang onto what we no longer need. We dwell on our inadequacies. We daydream ourselves into inaction. We fear our propensity to fail.

We don't have to be this way. There is a way to accept our imperfections while getting on with life, while working to achieve our goals using the flawed instruments of ourselves. And the by-product of this approach toward productive living is a rebuilt character, less neurotic misery, a genuine chance at success. It's worth a try. It requires purposeful attention and effort. But, as that Japanese physician named Morita put it, "Effort *is* Success."

So, Constructive Living is not really a method to cure anything; it is rather a means of acquiring life wisdom. It is applicable to everyone, acceptable to some, and applied by a few. You can usually tell who they are.

Let's get on with it.

PART I:

CONSTRUCTIVE LIVING
OBSERVATIONS

This section contains short essays about a variety of Constructive Living topics.

Bringing You Up to Date

A number of books have been written about Constructive Living. They include my own series: *Playing Ball on Running Water, Even in Summer the Ice Doesn't Melt, Water Bears No Scars, Constructive Living, The Quiet Therapies, Morita Psychotherapy,* and *Naikan Psychotherapy*. Perhaps you have read one or more of these books. In case you don't know much at all about Constructive Living, this brief section will outline some of the information contained in these earlier works.

Constructive Living is both a technique of psychotherapy and a practical way to live. It is built upon fundamental principles of human life. These principles were taught and practiced by a Japanese psychiatrist named Morita and a Japanese lay priest named Yoshimoto. The combining of Morita's therapy and Yoshimoto's Naikan was first undertaken in the West. We have developed and reinterpreted some elements of these enlightened lifeways to fit the needs of Westerners. Constructive Living never was Oriental mysticism. Even in its earliest forms in Japan it was positive, pragmatic, down-to-earth, everyday wisdom. It requires neither belief nor special skills. It contains simple advice and exercises to check out whether it fits with your experience, opportunities to determine its benefits, and limits.

Like much in life that is worthwhile, Constructive Living grows more from experiential understanding than from superficial intellectual knowledge. If you read about these methods and don't try to put any of the principles into practice, you would miss the point of learning about it. Constructive Living can help you develop a more productive, grateful, alert, and loving character no matter where you are starting. The investment of attention and effort will pay off. Don't believe me; give it a try and see for yourself.

Constructive Living is based upon ideas from Morita therapy and Naikan. Let's look at each of these systems of thought and action. We'll start with Morita's system.

MORITA'S LIFEWAY

This system takes a clear, hard look at what is possible and what is impossible in human life. It is impossible, for example, for us to control our feelings directly by our will. We cannot make ourselves feel confidence or love or courage by some direct effort of our minds. We cannot stop feelings of shyness or loneliness or grief or anxiety merely by wishing them to go away. So we have no responsibility for what we feel. We aren't bad for having sexy or hateful or depressed feelings. We aren't good for having noble feelings. How can we be morally responsible for what we can't control?

On the other hand, it is possible to be in some control of what we do (our behavior) no matter what we are feeling. We can accomplish much of what needs to be done in our lives even when our feelings are jumping about outside of our direct control. Furthermore, through our behavior we have some chance of indirectly influencing how we feel. For example, if you feel anxious about an upcoming job interview there are three major choices available. You can try to make yourself stop feeling anxious (impossible by your will, possible with enough alcohol or tranquilizers—but risky); you can skip the interview (and be weakened by your cowardly behavior); or you can go ahead with the interview all the while feeling anxious (the best chance, though not guaranteed, of getting the job).

Morita's system recommends accepting feelings as they are, without trying the impossible task of overcoming them, and going

DAVID K. REYNOLDS

on about doing what needs to be done. Morita observed that feelings fade over time unless we do something to restimulate them. Emotions (pleasant ones or unpleasant) never continue at their peak intensity for very long. As they wax and wane it is wiser to build life on steady, constructive behavior. Morita provided advice about paying attention to our changing world, noticing what needs to be done, and using each fresh moment to accomplish our purposes.

"Morita therapy is a character-building process developed in Japan in the early twentieth century. It strengthens those who practice it to surmount problems instead of trying to knock them down. In fact, the word often used in Japanese when doing this therapy is *norikoeru,* which is the same word one would use to indicate climbing over a wall. Isn't that the way many of your problems appear to you? Like walls? Not only the problems created by external circumstances, but also those fears and doubts and worries within. They, too, loom like walls between you and the achievement of the goals you have set for yourself. Yet, it's surprising how low a wall appears when you look back after scaling it. Sometimes the wall disappears entirely. But the strength and skill we develop in going over one wall prepares us for surmounting the next. Granted, some walls in the world we cannot tear down, but we can work hard at becoming better and better at climbing." (From *Playing Ball on Running Water,* p. 12.)

"You see, the fully functioning human being isn't someone who is utterly free of pain and happy all the time. Not at all. The mature human being goes about doing what needs to be done regardless of whether that person feels great or terrible. Knowing that you are that kind of person with that kind of self-control brings all the satisfaction and confidence you will ever need. Even on days when the satisfaction and confidence just aren't there, you can get the job done anyway." (From *Constructive Living,* p. 5.)

"What is certain is that I am sometimes this, sometimes that. Sometimes pleased, sometimes not; sometimes confident, sometimes not; sometimes compassionate, sometimes not. The ice doesn't melt at my whim. It doesn't melt no matter how well I understand its origins or believe I understand its origins. It may not melt despite my persistent efforts to change the circumstances that I believe to be maintaining it. In such cases what else is there to do but shiver and go on about living?" (From *Even in Summer the Ice Doesn't Melt*, p. 22.)

So, the life strategy of Morita involves accepting feelings as they are (not ignoring them, not pretending they are always pleasant, not necessarily always wanting them or liking them), being aware of our purposes, and acting constructively to achieve our goals. The emphasis is on the naturalness of our feelings, the inevitability of constant change, the need to conduct ourselves responsibly in difficult times as well as easy ones. We learn to keep alert to what Reality (read God here, if you prefer) is sending us that needs to be done. We become the means by which Reality gets things accomplished.

YOSHIMOTO'S LIFEWAY

Naikan is a Japanese word meaning literally "inside observation" or "introspection." Yoshimoto was refining his method in the 1930s, about the time when Morita died. Naikan focuses on the concrete, specific ways in which we are supported by people and other elements of our world. When we truly recognize the details of this ongoing support we feel gratitude for receiving it, guilt for failing to repay it, and a desire to give ourselves away in service to others.

Neurotic suffering grows from self-centeredness. Naikan, like Morita's lifeway, helps us to pry our attention away from our exclusive self-focus. While Morita is directing our attention toward what Reality is bringing us moment by moment, Naikan prods us to see how Reality is serving us moment by moment. One's past is reinterpreted and unnecessary neurotic suffering is reduced.

"However, relief from these aspects of human suffering are, again, merely circumstantial by-products of the working out of naikan's genuine purpose—changing the client's attitude toward his past, both distant and recent. The gratitude and sense of having been loved in spite of one's errors expresses itself in joyful, self-sacrificing behavior. The ailments may continue, they may require

DAVID K. REYNOLDS

struggle or tolerance, other physical treatment, or adaptation to a restricted life-style. But the context of the suffering is reformed by naikan. One does not—one did not—suffer alone. Naikan promises such discoveries of self. It would appear that to a considerable degree naikan delivers what it offers to the earnest client." (From *The Quiet Therapies,* pp. 64–65.)

"Naikan is bubbling feelings, the murky past, suppressed memories. It is charged with emotion; it generates emotion in rather the opposite way from Morita's method, which keeps grounding the charge of emotion in reality. Naikan taps the energy we use to hide our dark side from others and from ourselves. It turns that energy of camouflage into gratitude, repentance, and an awareness that we were loved, are loved in spite of our imperfections." (From *Naikan Psychotherapy,* p. 3.)

PUTTING THESE LIFEWAYS TOGETHER

Constructive Living combines the insights of these two life-styles into a balanced approach to life in this modern world. The cool pragmatism of Morita's method complements the warm emotions of Naikan. Homework assignments may involve saying "thank you" ten times a day to a quarreling spouse (Naikan's attention to services from others) whether you feel gratitude or not (Morita's action regardless of uncontrollable feelings).

Similarly, a shy student may be asked to clean up trash in a local park (Naikan's service in repayment of our debt to society) all the while feeling conspicuous and embarrassed (Morita's acceptance of feelings while doing what needs doing).

Perhaps I have written enough here to give you a foothold for scaling what is to follow. Compare what you read here with your own life experience, not with what you have read about psychology in textbooks. I think you will find no *Japanese* wisdom in these pages, but *human* wisdom.

WHAT'S NEW?

What changes take place when we embark on this journey of Constructive Living? What new sights and insights greet us?

First, we begin to see our limitations and strengths from a new perspective. What we are, we are. There is no need to eliminate our upsetting feelings. They fade into background as we zero in on the problem of paralyzed behavior. Purpose begins to emerge into the foreground of our attention. And the behavior that walks us toward our purposes absorbs our interest.

We begin to expect change rather than the same old story of continuing misery. As we begin to see the results of this life-style, we begin to look forward to even greater personal growth.

We create a new self. This process is more active than discovering a new self. It is not as if this new self were there all along and our eyes were closed to it. Rather, our efforts carve the living beauty of a new self out of the dead wood of old habits and old thought patterns.

Playing by the Book

When I was young, I had the naive notion that if I played life by the book everything had to turn out well. If I made the sacrifices and worked hard and kept my nose clean I would "deserve" the rewards that would come my way. Reality soon showed me the foolishness of such thinking. A model family that prayed together failed to stay together. As a scholar I published and, nevertheless, perished (as an academic) in a wave of university budget cuts. How troubling. What could I count on? Life wasn't "fair."

I began to look around with "new eyes" and discovered that such obvious injustices weren't my lot alone. Wonderful and kind and productive friends died of cancer. Children with fine upbringing unraveled their lives with drugs. Companies with well-designed products and excellent customer support went under during rough economic times. No fairy-tale outcome was assured, no matter what the input.

So where can we put our trust? Certainly not in outcomes, in results. No matter how hard we try, no matter how diligently we pursue a course, there is no guarantee that a malignancy or a flood or an earthquake or the stroke of a lawmaker's pen or a recession or someone else's infatuation won't come along to ruin the hoped-for fruits of our efforts. No guarantee at all.

Is there nothing trustworthy, then? Yes, there is something that we can depend upon. It is the doing itself. The doing, the effort, the acting on what is right there before our eyes that needs our attention—that is what we can rely on. We can trust proper action to produce proper character. We can turn ourselves into the people we are capable of becoming by living the way we are capable of living.

To live in such a way doesn't remove our hopes and desires for satisfying outcomes. We still long for successful results. We still hurt when life isn't turning out exactly as we had hoped it would. Nevertheless, whatever the results of our actions, we reap the benefit and satisfaction of doing our doings well.

The Third Stage

Thus far in my writings I have only described the first two stages of development for students of Constructive Living. In the first stage the suffering students learn to carry out tasks in order to be distracted from their symptoms. In other words, they vacuum the carpet in order to distract themselves from their anxiety. In the second stage, the students learn to carry out tasks just because the tasks need to be done. Anxious or not, they vacuum the rug because the rug is dirty.

We call the first stage "feeling-centered." It is not fundamentally different from the condition of neurotic suffering. There is some relief from anxiety because the student has learned the tactic of distraction through activities. However, the fundamental attitude toward feelings has not changed. The students continue to evaluate their lives in terms of whether they are hurting or not.

We call the second stage "purpose-centered." The attitude toward activities has changed. Tasks are no longer seen as primarily a means of escape from suffering. Moment-by-moment tasks are accomplished just because they need doing. Doing them well becomes the measure of life success, and not the absence of anxiety, fear, or other unpleasant feelings.

Now for the third stage. Let me begin by pointing out that achieving this stage isn't necessary for everyone. We can get through life satisfactorily and productively in the second stage of purpose focus. In fact, people who live pretty consistently in the second stage, without often slipping back into feeling-centered living, are especially accomplished people. There are a very few people who move on to another level, however. It is a level at which you might say that Reality just gets its tasks done.

At the second stage I answer a letter because that is what needs doing, that is what the situation calls for in that particular moment. But it is still me answering the letter. There is some satisfaction in the small achievement of replying to the letter. We say that such constructive activity helps to build our character, self-confidence, and a healthy self-image.

Although the attitude in the second stage is purpose-focused, it is still self-centered, in a way. It is *my* character, *my* self-confidence, *my* self-image, *my* satisfaction that comes from doing a task well. At the third stage of Constructive Living we see ourselves as just another way that Reality gets its jobs done. More accurately, there is just vacuuming, just letter writing, and so forth. We see ourselves as just another aspect of the situation that is occurring at this moment. We are just another means of achieving Reality's purposes. There is no more credit due me for writing a letter than due the pen or the paper (or the person who wrote the letter to which the reply will be sent). There is just letter writing, just now.

The distinction between hedonism and altruism disappears at this level. In giving to another part of this circumstance (you) I give to this part of this circumstance (me), or, better yet, the circumstance gives to the circumstance. That is, the circumstance is just moving objects and energies around.

This third level may appear to be rather mystical or philosophical or religious at first glance. But it is, in fact, the most truthful and realistic approach to living if you examine everyday activities closely. Nevertheless, few people seem to adopt this way of looking at the world, and these only for relatively short periods of time. The major pitfall of making efforts to achieve this most realistic of perspectives is that of slipping into the mistaken belief that one must withdraw from the world (through meditation, for example) in order to achieve it.

DAVID K. REYNOLDS

Look around you. You are autonomous, you believe. You have free will. You make choices. Where do your decisions come from? Find the first glimmering of a choice in your mind. Trace back a decision until you find the first moment of its appearance in your awareness. What was its source?

Can you see yourself as part of this scene in this play that Reality is producing and directing? Just another character, no more nor less important than the script or the stage props or the stage itself. Just another aspect that allows the show to go on.

There is no need to aim for stage three of Constructive Living. If you keep your eyes open you may eventually arrive there from stage two. There is no way to describe fully the experience of stage three moments with words. It is rather like trying to describe the taste of an orange using only watercolors. Words are unsatisfactory when we try to communicate about such topics as suffering, death, autonomy, choice, stage three, and the like. Words are even dangerous at such times because we are deluded into believing that we understand something that we don't really understand just because we have talked about it.

It is unnecessary, and even harmful, to stop washing the dishes in order to search for stage three. The dishes need to be washed. The dishes deserve to be washed. Withdrawing ourselves from the dishes isolates us back into self-centeredness. When we fully attend to dishwashing, just this dish now, then there will be times when there is only dishwashing going on—a taste of stage three.

Work and Life Meaning

In *The Environment Game* British author Nigel Calder notes that the concept of work was invented to fit the tedium of agriculture. Gratification from earlier hunting and gathering ways was more immediately connected with effort. Agriculture required days of repetitious effort and delays until harvest time. Calder suggests that with the coming of automation we shall find the concept of work useless.

I think that we can already see a trend appearing, not toward dropping the word *work* from our vocabulary, but toward broadening it to include all sorts of meaningful activities. For example, a certain amount of work is conducted during lunches and at the golf course. Hobbyists sometimes reap great profits from their productions and collections. And it is unclear whether professional sports figures can be said to be "working" as they play before their fans.

Clearly, in the sixty-year history of Constructive Living we can see a trend toward the broadening of the concept of work. In modern Constructive Living we use games and singing and a variety of other sorts of mind-focusing activities, as well, to develop a constructive life-style. In the early days of Constructive Living most of the focus was on manual labor, often labor that was connected with the soil.

There is some genuine value in digging and planting and

weeding and harvesting from the soil. We learn patience. We learn the rhythm of natural phenomena. We use our bodies in physical activity. We reap the benefits of our labor and the labor of those who help us in the concrete form of food or flowers. We can use this form of work to serve others and ourselves. We learn gratitude to the sun, mild weather, water, and human effort.

But, of course, Constructive Living can be learned and practiced on a golf course or on a subway as well as it can be learned in a garden. And as attitudes and activities change in modern times, people seem to prefer broader expressions of Constructive Living than in manual toil alone.

Dr. Takehisa Kora points out that some of our dissatisfaction with narrow notions of work comes from our seeing the products we work on thrown away without thought in this consumer society. The fruits of our labor may be taken for granted and wasted by many members of our society. Thus, the meaning of our effort seems to be diluted.

Joy can be found in even physical, repetitious labor when we can see the results of our work, when our work produces beauty (a tulip or a painting, for example), and when others value and appreciate our work. There is something intrinsically rewarding about viewing the fruits of our efforts.

So, work is coming to mean any meaningful activity, any purposeful activity. This interest in knowing one's purpose, and making constructive efforts toward achieving it is central to Constructive Living. This approach to life is right in step with our changing times and our broadening of the concept of work.

Numbers Games

1. TWO WAYS

There are two ways to fail. One is to fail while trying. The other is to fail effortlessly.

There are two ways to try. One is to try. The other is to try to try.

There are two ways to change. One is to expect and accept change. The other is to resist inevitable change.

There are two ways to feel—with and without giving yourself permission to feel.

There are two ways to approach a standard of excellence—lower the standard or raise the performance.

There are two ways to be a hero. One way is to imagine oneself a hero. The other is to live like one.

There are two ways to live a marriage—with gratitude or with grit.

2. FOUR BASES FOR DECISIONS

Rev. Shue Usami of Senkobo Temple in Japan teaches the four traditional Buddhist bases for evaluating behavior. They are: time, place, point of view, and amount. Time and place are obvious. Driving a car is appropriate when going to the airport but not when fleeing from an auto accident. Point of view has to do with one's station in life. When one adopts a role or accepts a job offer, one is benefitted in certain ways, but one also accepts certain limitations on behavior. It is proper to get up in the morning (feeling like it or not), dress in a suitable uniform, and report to work at a particular time if one is a postal employee or a surgical nurse. Amount is also important. How much one eats, how much one works and plays, how much one spends on a gift, a car, a house—all these are moral issues.

Note that I make no attempt to define what is the proper amount for *you* to spend on a car or house. Each of us makes that evaluation for himself or herself. But, although the moral boundaries are defined by each individual, the choices are all moral ones. They are not economic or pragmatic alone, for example. *Every* act is right/wrong, good/bad in terms of place, point of view, and amount.

3. SEVEN WAYS TO BE MISERABLE

Here, I am borrowing in part from a fine article by Dr. Takehisa Kora published in Japanese in the May, 1986 issue of *Seikatsu no Hakken* magazine. I have combined and rearranged items from his list and added several items of my own, but both lists were written in the same spirit of Constructive Living. There follows a list of methods you can adopt to make yourself miserable.

1. Unnecessary comparison. The first item on my list of ways to assure misery in one's life is to habitually make comparisons in negative ways. I can't play tennis like a professional or memorize as well as I did when I was younger. Others are stronger and wiser and wealthier and more powerful and more artistic and more clever than I. Some people seem to be happier and more relaxed and more confident than I. Such comparisons are unnecessary and lead to lack of confidence and self esteem.

Although these comparisons may be accurate, they lead to nothing constructive. Another truth is that I can achieve what I can achieve. When I put out effort to make a garden or a book or an orderly and clean room, I can take some pride in the accomplishment, regardless of how much better someone else might do it.

Jealousy comes from a similar sort of comparison, at least in part. We compare what is with the ideal, with what we think others have, with what we consider is our due. And we feel deprived and possessive and anxious about what might be.

Absolutism and idealism are other versions of improper comparison. We can never have absolute safety, perfect freedom from anxiety, or complete harmony of body and mind. To avoid the very possibility of a traffic accident we would have to stay home all the time, and staying home doesn't guarantee safety. Household accidents, earthquakes, tornadoes, fires, and the like threaten our safety even at home. Living involves risks and threats, fuzziness and rough approximations, and imperfection.

Similarly, people with excessively high standards and ideals find themselves and others lacking when compared with the desired perfection. If they aren't Olympics level sportspeople or if they don't get 100 percent scores on exams they are upset with themselves.

Even comparisons with people less fortunate than ourselves can produce misery. I know people who survived major disasters and feel guilty that *they* were saved and not some neighbor or friend or relative.

Perhaps we humans cannot altogether avoid comparing our lot with that of others or with some absolute or ideal. But we can minimize ruminating about the comparisons in ways that have negative effects on our lives. Doing well what is right in front of me right now takes a lot of purposeful attention. There is little time for dwelling on pointless comparisons.

2. *Fighting reality.* It is foolish to disregard or struggle against the reality of what is. A much better strategy is to accept what is and work to change it in desirable ways.

Let's consider some of the ways people disregard reality. Some people try to accelerate the natural flow of time. We know, for example, that the feelings of abandonment and anger following a divorce or separation or job loss will fade over time if left alone without restimulating them. But some people try to rush this natural healing process with tranquilizers or alcohol. Similarly, if you lose a moderate amount of money in a business deal, the initial intense feelings of loss and failure will predictably diminish over time. Trying to hasten reality's natural pace only produces undesired side effects.

Another way some people ignore the realities of life is by exceeding natural limits and boundaries. Even in ordinarily positive areas of life, like work and study and eating and playing, people may go to excess and reap misery as a result. There are proper amounts and times for our activities. Discovering them and abiding by them are tasks prudently observed by mature individuals.

People sometimes try to leap beyond the boundaries of their abilities or stations in life. We admire those who succeed, and we encourage individuals to press and expand their limits. But to try the impossible, and fail, again and again seems less reasonable than reexamining one's goals and trying to achieve something that may be difficult but is at least possible. There must be a balance between aspirations and situations and abilities if we are to avoid unnecessary misery in life.

Reality brings change, all kinds of change. We can count on it. People who rail against any kind of change are doomed to lives of dissatisfaction. But change brings opportunities as well as inconvenience. The word "challenge" contains the word "change." Without change there would be no challenge.

3. *Self focus.* There is a constellation of traits involving selfishness and self-centeredness, unreadiness to love, and dependency, which conspire in the lives of some to produce suffering. Kora points out that mature individuals love not only people but also Nature and ideas among other things.

Self-centered individuals lack trust in others, evaluate situations and people in terms of what's in it for them. In their efforts to assure themselves that their own needs will be met they find themselves depending on others while doubting others' abilities to meet their needs. They pace their lives in terms of how they are feeling at the moment. If they feel the slightest headache or psychological unreadiness they cancel dates and appointments without a thought for the convenience of others. The activities of their day revolve around the capricious ups and downs of their minds.

It is no wonder that such people often see themselves as helpless. They are pushed about by their desires (again, desires aren't bad in themselves) and by their efforts to get themselves and others to build lives around their momentary whims and passing fancies.

4. *Purposeless living.* In Kora's list of ways to assure misery he includes an item of not working. I have broadened the idea somewhat to include the lack of all sorts of purposeful behavior. People who have no meaningful behavior to pull them into life are, for the moment, headed for misery and some sort of death (physical, psychological, or social). Purpose pulls us into life. Compare the person who is actively engaged in some absorbing project with the person who merely fills time with meaningless activity.

5. *Unhealthy life-style.* People who mistreat their bodies pay the price. It is as simple as that. Their bodies may be genetically equipped to resist obvious illnesses for a long time, but they operate at less than optimal capacity and eventually succumb.

What needs to be done may be to find alternative activities to smoking and drinking alcohol, to get more exercise or sleep, to eat a proper diet at regular times, and so forth. Mental health, too, can be promoted by various sorts of reading, hobbies, social activities, and the like. To neglect a balance in one's mind/body health is to invite misery.

6. *Negativism.* Such negative activities as complaining, criticizing, and gossiping foster a pessimistic outlook that, in one way or another, turns itself back on the violator of Constructive Living principles. Complainers keep drawing their own attention to their own misery, thus exaggerating it. Meanwhile, their constant complaints alienate those around them.

Critical people operate in a world of faults and dissatisfaction which includes their own self-image. They criticize themselves, too. The habit of looking at the world with narrowed, negatively evaluating eyes makes appreciating the positive events of life difficult. Success doesn't fit their frame of mind. The person with many pessimistic moments feels uncomfortable when things *seem to be* going well.

7. *Lack of gratitude and appreciation for "being lived."* I have written elsewhere that I have yet to meet a neurotically suffering

individual who is filled with gratitude for the supports of life—
"being lived." Gratitude and misery are antagonistic.

Gratitude and anxiety are antagonistic, too. They emerge from
different worlds and different perspectives. Anxiety is inner directed. It focuses on what is happening or what will happen to
me. *My* discomfort is primary, *my* problem the center of the universe.

On the other hand, gratitude is outer directed. It focuses on
what OTHERS are doing, have done, and will do in my behalf. It
is *their* contribution, *their* effort, *their* kindness that is the center of
attention.

Neurosis is fundamentally inner-focused attention. It feeds on
and generates anxiety. Actions that stimulate gratitude counter
neurotic tendencies.

Gratitude is a natural response to keeping our eyes open.
When we aren't distracted by the various blinders our self-centeredness imposes on our sight we need only look about to find
the myriads of ways Reality (in the form of people and energy and
objects, for example) supports us. Our very breath is borrowed
from the air that surrounds us.

We can assure ourselves misery by believing that we got where
we are solely by our own efforts.

Successful Fools

The Japanese psychiatrist Morita wrote, "While considering that there is something wrong with your mind, while feeling pessimistic about yourself, just keep working your mind vigorously." Here is a viable alternative to the strange Western advice to try to make yourself feel confident and successful when you don't and you're not.

Can you see the reasonable nature of this approach? You don't need to try to convince yourself that you are OK and that all is well in your life or your mind. It's quite all right to recognize your failures and limitations and anxieties and obsessions, and even to feel hopeless and pessimistic about them. After all, that *is* the way you feel about them sometimes. But Morita's advice doesn't stop with merely accepting the reality that we can't run away from anyway. He advises us to keep on working those imperfect, distressed minds vigorously. By working our minds vigorously he means to keep noticing what Reality sends our way and to attend carefully to doing well those moment-by-moment activities of which our lives are composed. Feel despair but take out the trash. Be pessimistic but plan your vacation. While feeling depressed shave. Walk the depths of hopelessness but prepare and show up for the job interview. While berating yourself for this morning's mistake don't miss the freeway turnoff.

It is quite all right to be the fool who lives life well.

Garden Notes

EYES OPEN

There are always weeds hanging around the borders of the garden, waiting to invade. Like the barbarians along the boundaries of a civilization, like the delusions and misunderstandings at the boundaries of our enlightenment, they must be observed and challenged if we are to maintain our vigor and strength.

As I kneel and pull at weeds in one small corner of the garden, I come to discover large weeds I hadn't noticed before. It takes time to understand even a small corner of a small plot of earth. Time and attention, just putting myself in one place, keeping busy, keeping my eyes open. How varied and instructive is our world!

WORKOUT

Gardening provides a natural physical workout suited to the exercise needs of just about anyone. If your situation permits, I highly recommend gardening as a hobby. It seems strange to me that some people hire gardeners and then join health clubs in order to get enough exercise. A vegetable, herb, and flower garden can provide beauty, organically-grown food, the occasion for exercise, and a subtle sort of—well—companionship.

The Costliness of Wealth

There is a price paid for affluence. Luxury has its costs, not only in terms of money. In this short essay I do not recommend that we abandon our hard-earned gains and retreat to a life of poverty. I meet too many people who strive for wealth because they haven't found any other meaningful goal for their lives. They aim for dollars by default. And, for some, affluence is grossly overpriced. Let's consider how.

A life of ease is often accompanied by the failure to value and fully use objects, energy, opportunities. It is so convenient to dispose of things impulsively, to consume without thought, to put off until later, to let others do our work for us.

Gratitude for the smallest of objects, the briefest of services, begins to fade quickly. We take from the world as though it were our due.

There is a tendency among some who are financially comfortable to dabble in self-development. They flit from one trendy growth technique to another, for they soon become tired of any path. They learn the jargon and the exercises, then they move on. They want to know about enlightened living, but refuse the sacrifices necessary to live it.

It is a waste of time to aim for only a taste of Constructive Living. You don't put your toe in the water and consider yourself able to swim. As in many areas of life, a little knowledge can be dangerous. It isn't unusual to meet people who have nibbled on est and rolfing and assertiveness training, encounter groups, and gestalt groups. They have tasted transactional, transpersonal, and transcendental snacks. They are looking for another self-growth tidbit.

The telephone number of the ToDo Institute is not in the Los Angeles telephone directory. I don't want to be bothered by dilettantish faddists. Those who search with some persistence are able to track us down. Those with mild curiosity drop out before wasting their time or ours. The method is not foolproof—some get through who will drop out soon, others who would have done well never get through to us. We do what we can.

Some people depend upon wealth (read: a steady job, savings, a solid business, a well-heeled mate, their investments) to save them. And why not? The fruits of their labor or luck appear before their eyes each day. Economic considerations are molding their world.

Another cost of this focus on wealth is the necessity of keeping a concerned eye on keeping it or increasing it. Long hours are invested in watching stock prices, talking with brokers, switching to the accounts with highest returns. To do less is to be foolish, financially speaking. That time and that attention won't be returned to the investor. I am not saying that they are wasted. I am saying that they are invested with a personal cost.

The immediate purposes of life, the obvious right-up-front values that we hold (should we take the time to consider them), are pushed into tomorrow as we work at becoming/staying well-to-do. It is easy to lose perspective in our purposes as we push for more and more.

Beware the poverty that accompanies wealth!

DAVID K. REYNOLDS

Fitting Circumstances and People

Why is it that little children love to draw and color pictures but few adults enjoy this pastime? Four- and five-year-old children are forever pestering their parents for paper on which to demonstrate their artistry. But by the time they reach the sixth grade, only those who are specializing in art seem to enjoy making pictures as much as they did when younger. And few adults draw, color, or paint unless it is their profession. Why?

One reason seems to be the critical judgment of others. Teachers evaluate children's drawings, usually in terms of what the teachers like or think realistic. Children learn to draw in conformity with what their teachers and their parents will praise.

The joy declines as the awareness of others' evaluations grows. It is important, I believe, to recognize the child's individuality in drawing without trying to make it fit some absolute standard of realism. Children usually do what needs doing, naturally. Their actions may look like failure to adults, but their failures, too, are the roots of learning. Rather than offering an adult criticism of children's drawings, it is better to ask them in detail about what they have drawn—and learn from the children's explanations.

I have written that there is only one best way to carry out an activity at any given time. There is a best way for me to brush my teeth this morning. It may not be the same way as the best way to brush my teeth last night or yesterday morning. But any other way is less than the best, less than what needs to be done.

This best way fits not only the immediate circumstances (Where is the toothbrush? Is there running water? Where is the toothpaste? Where to place the toothpaste cap while brushing?), but also the best way fits the person. A child's best way is not the same as an adult's. Your best way is not mine.

Sometimes we try to make children conform to our adult ways. Drawing pictures is a good example of the unnecessary pressures put on children by adults to act like grownups.

DAVID K. REYNOLDS

Misalignments

Ten years or so ago I wrote a small book with a vignette about a little girl in Kamakura who was crying to be allowed back into her house. She had done something wrong, and her punishment was to be put outside the house. She stood pounding on the front door, tearfully begging to be allowed into the house. I contrasted this Japanese girl's plight with that of the American child who is forced to stay in his or her room as punishment. The American child is not allowed out of the house. The Japanese girl saw her mother and her home as the source of life's rewards. The American child sees the unrestrained freedom of play outside the home as desirable. The reality is somewhat more complicated than this simple contrast, but the story called attention to some differing tendencies between the two countries that seem to be valid.

Later, I saw the same vignette in the writings of a Japan specialist. I was not quoted or credited. For a moment I was miffed, then I recalled that the credit for the story wasn't mine. Should I have credited the little girl? Her family? Those who taught me the Japanese language so that I could understand what she was saying between sobs? The editor and publisher of the book in which the vignette appeared? The government agency that funded that first period of research in Japan? Without any one of these people (and a host of others) there would have been no story to tell. How narrowly self-centered to think that the story could be "mine."

What about *your* marriage, *your* project, *your* child, *your* self-development, *your* success?

I made a similar mistake the other day as I turned off the cold water. I started to turn to a brief task while allowing the water to run in the sink. Then I stopped and turned off the water first, thinking all the while what a conscientious person I am. It is wrong to refrain from wasting water because I want to consider myself a good person. The reality is that I'm not, particularly. It is proper to turn off the water because the water "deserves" to be used carefully, with attention (and, when the feeling wells up, with gratitude). We do what is right because it is right—not because we are fine people, not because God will punish or reward us, not because of sheer habit, not to show off our proper upbringing, not to atone for our sins—just because it is right.

I began reading David Viscott's book about how to conduct the business aspects of psychotherapy. In *Taking Care of Business*, Viscott honestly and straightforwardly points out that psychotherapy is a business, and he goes on to offer advice on how to run that business properly and successfully. His candor is admirable.

The most useful revelation for me was that I am not in the business of psychotherapy. I am in the business of trying to repay the world for my existence. It is nice to receive fees and royalties and honoraria. But Constructive Living is more important than a means of making a livelihood. It is the means of making a life, a whole life. And the financial aspect of that whole life waxes and wanes in importance from moment to moment. The debts I owe aren't merely financial. Constructive Living is more than making a living; it's my life.

On General Principles

Professor Anees Sheikh tells the story of a young student from India who came to visit the United States. He was accustomed to brewing tea from loose tea leaves, so when a teabag was given to him he began to tear it open. His host told him that in America we simply drop the whole teabag into our cup. So, having learned his lesson, he picked up a packet of sugar and . . .

What the student did makes some sense. He continued to operate on the principle of "not tearing." But the results weren't as expected. His behavior turned out to be unrealistic. We need to keep checking out what we do against the standards of Reality. But some people try to figure out much of reality in their minds, without acting on it. Because they fail to observe what really is, they expect Reality to be like their fantasies and imaginings.

Toraware is an important word in Constructive Living. It means being caught or obsessed. The word is often used to describe the sense of being hung up on neurotic symptoms. Yozo Hasegawa, the director of the Morita mental health organization in Japan, has shown that the concept of toraware can be useful to everyone. He talked about the obsession of some salaried men with their work and the similarity of that obsession to being "caught" by neurotic symptoms. Both neurotic people and workaholics show a kind of inflexibility, a poor adaptation to the reality that presents itself to them. People can be obsessed with all sorts of things—by succeeding, by making money, by being in love, by their faults, by studying, by sex, by neurotic symptoms, by their work, by self-development, and so forth. None of these interests is bad in itself—there is nothing wrong, for example, with wanting to be successful or free of faults—it is the being caught, the toraware, which freezes attention on the obsession and turns us away from the "sunao" or open acceptance of Reality that *is* the problem.

I would suggest that we go even further theoretically. It is not the neurotic symptoms that we correct by Constructive Living, but the toraware itself. The symptoms are no better or worse than the desire to succeed, the impulse to study, or the dream of buying a new home. It is *the obsession* with any of these that needs to be corrected. The obsession narrows the thinking and separates the person from reality. When we focus exclusively on an obsession (such as trying to get rid of neurotic symptoms or trying to succeed in our profession) we cannot see the reality around us, so we cannot see what properly needs to be done in each moment. It is the toraware, *the obsession itself,* that is the difficulty.

People can be stuck on images or stereotypes, too. This perseveration is a sort of toraware. For example, many Japanese seem to think that foreigners must be tall, sexy, assertive, open, drinkers of alcohol and coffee, eaters of great quantities of bread. Someone once made an especially long futon quilted bedding for me because I am a foreigner. Salespeople suggest large sizes in shirts and suits and slacks because I am a foreigner. In fact, I am about the same height as the average Japanese male, wear medium-size Japanese clothing, rarely eat bread, and rarely drink alcohol or coffee. Many foreigners don't fit the stereotype Japanese have of them. Just as many Japanese don't fit the stereotype Americans have of them. Most Japanese don't eat sushi every day, rarely wear geta (wooden clogs), and don't carry a camera around every day. Some Japanese sleep in a bed, not on a floor mat and futon; their homes have carpets as well as tatami-mat rooms, and so forth.

There are stereotypes of women, too, that produce a kind of toraware. Many Japanese people think that women should be housewives, staying at home to raise children, shy, uninterested in politics or economics, experts in shopping and flower arrangement and tea ceremony. Actually, many women in Japan are now working outside the home (at least part-time), some are choosing not to marry, some are successful in business and politics and sports. Some women are choosing to move beyond the narrow limits of stereotypes. So the stereotypes will change little by little there just as they have been changing in the United States.

General principles can be useful tools for direction in everyday life. But we must periodically check them against Reality. We cannot afford to let ourselves become rigidly attached to principles, attitudes, and ideas that no longer fit Reality (if they ever did). Constructive Living aims not so much at perfect consistency or unchanging perfection, but at flexible, natural realism.

No Small Matter

THE TRICKLE-DOWN EFFECT

Constructive Living trickles down into the smallest detail of daily life. Students are likely to find themselves turning off lights when not in use, using heaters less during the night, noticing the efforts of others that go into their daily bath. They notice that they are cleaning and polishing their shoes regularly, brushing their teeth more carefully, considering their pets' feelings/needs more, appreciating their food more, giving to others not because they have become different from them but because they see how much like them they are, becoming aware of the "aliveness" of food and machines and furniture and water and energy of all sorts.

In fact, only when it has begun to trickle down into the small crevices of daily thoughts and activities can Constructive Living really be said to have taken hold in one's life. Grand insight and deepened understanding are but momentary phenomena. Our existence is constructed on the bedrock of moment-by-moment living.

RUBBISH

Attention to the detail of what we do helps sharpen our minds and refine our lives. I sometimes advise my students to make their trash beautiful. When you unwrap the paper from your hamburger what do you do with the paper? When you remove chopsticks from their paper wrapper do you wad up the wrapper and leave the unsightly thing on the table? How does your trash look sitting in front of your house or apartment building? How about the waste receptacles in your home?

Twenty years ago, as I first walked the residential areas of Tokyo, I was struck by the neatness of the trash set out for collection. Much of the garbage was wrapped neatly and tied with ribbons, looking more like something to be given as Christmas presents than like something to be abandoned. Even today, as Japanese finish their box lunches on the trains, they neatly tie up the empty boxes in the paper wrapping and deposit tidy bundles into the trash. Some Japanese fold the paper chopstick wrappers to make a functional stand to lay the chopsticks on when not using them. Almost everyone can fold the wrapper into a flattened form of half knot that is very presentable and decorative.

So what? Who cares? Trash is trash, isn't it? Once it is picked up and out of sight the problem of unsightliness disappears, doesn't it? Maybe not. If we take seriously an attitude of appreciation for concrete services from our world then wrappers and bags and rubber bands and staples and the like deserve some appreciation, as well. What is now trash was once our servant. It deserves respectful treatment. Sound strange? I wonder.

Rubbish, too, merits our concerned attention.

WALKING

To watch a Zen master or a Kabuki actor or a classical Japanese dancer walk is to watch a lesson about living. The step is purposeful; the feet are placed one before the other with attention; balance is maintained throughout the stride. Walking becomes more than merely getting from one place to another. This taken-for-granted means of locomotion becomes an exercise of attention and character development.

It takes no great skill to make some educated guesses about people by watching the way they walk. There are mincers and swaggerers and prancers and totterers. But the way one walks need not be merely an *indication* of one's character and physical

DAVID K. REYNOLDS

condition, it can be a *determiner* of character and physical condition. Use your walk to develop purpose, confidence, awareness, and health. Attend to walking well.

Walking is more than getting from here to there.

COFFEE

Coffee or tea or plain hot water are warming, soothing, stimulating. Preparing and serving a hot drink can be automatic or engrossing, sloppy or artistic, character-eroding or character-building.

More than once I've drawn attention to the Japanese tea ceremony. The ceremony is simply the preparation and serving and drinking of a bitter form of green tea. How mundane! Yet how exquisite! Exquisite because the movements and attitudes have been refined over generations and over years of practice by skilled participants so that every movement is choreographed for simplicity and grace.

How do you prepare and pour your coffee? How do you measure out sugar and cream? How do you stir? How do you raise the cup to your lips? Have you considered the behaviors and attitudes with which you participate in the simple ceremony of coffee drinking? From the moment of deciding to drink, through heating the water and taking the cup from the cupboard, until the cup is washed and put away, there is much to fill attention. When carried out properly, drinking a cup of coffee is no small thing.

ET CETERA

There is no need to detail the important elements of making a bed, writing a letter, dusting, dictating a memo, washing one's hands, brushing one's teeth, carrying grocery bags from the garage to the house, hanging up clothes, and the like. Each activity carries its own importance. Each offers the opportunity to build character. But we must engage in attentively putting away the groceries because they deserve being put away in that fashion. If we try to put away the groceries carefully with the sole purpose of improving ourselves we run the risk of losing sight of the more important Reality—that the groceries need to be put away. The focus needs to be on the groceries, not on ourselves.

The by-product, then, of this aesthetic and purposeful action is the creation of an aesthetic and purposeful self. Again, attention to these small tasks is no small matter.

DAVID K. REYNOLDS

Healthy Pain

No one likes pain. Most of us have wished for its absence at one time or another in our lives. But the fact of the matter is that not only is some pain in life unavoidable, it is actually necessary for our growth. The process of surmounting discomfort provides special opportunities for personal development.

It isn't pleasant to be wrong. There are some words I misspelled for at least twenty years before someone pointed out those mistakes to me: "questionnaire" and "souvenir," for example. I foolishly thought that "souvenir" was misspelled in the small dictionary when I checked on it. It was embarrassing to discover these errors. But the discomfort of finding yet another imperfection was a necessary element of correcting these mistakes. As Fujita (1986, p. 47) put it, "Contradiction and conflict not only give rise to mental suffering but also provide the material that the mind consolidates to create harmony, stability and rhythm in living. Without the presence of contradiction and conflict there can be no mental growth."

When life (Reality) isn't going as we hoped or expected there is distress but also something to be learned, something different that needs doing. We must develop tolerance for a certain degree of suffering in order to benefit from these lessons from Reality. People who try to flee (into tranquilizers, alcohol, divorce, resignation, dropping out, or whatever) at the first signs of Reality-cramps miss the lessons and growth that come from endurance.

I am not suggesting that all pain is wonderful, that we should stoically endure whatever agony comes our way with no attempts to alleviate our suffering. To suggest such would be foolishness in several senses of that word. At the very least, no one would seriously adopt such advice for long. However, I am suggesting here that growth results not from some forever-smooth path of tranquility leading up the smooth slopes of a wisdom-forested mountain. Climbing over and around boulders, leaping chasms, fording rivers, and some dusty, sweaty insect-bitten distress are part of the journey toward self-development. Those who turn around to play in the lush fields at the foot of the mountain never get to see the views from higher up.

The stronger our desires, the higher our aspirations, the steeper is our path and the more pain/anxiety we endure. The more we want that dinner party to go well, the more we worry and anticipate all sorts of potential problems. The greater our desire to advance up the corporate ladder the more we sense our own handicaps and possible interference from others. The higher our goals for academic excellence the more we are aware of our own limitations of energy and intellect. The desire to succeed is inevitably accompanied by pain. Failure or even anticipated potential failure is painful in direct proportion to our wishes to succeed.

I would be the last person to advise giving up our desires for success in order to avoid the accompanying pain. Our success drive comes from our desires to live well, to live up to our potential, to survive (in physical, psychological, spiritual, and social senses). They are fine as they are. Anyway, even if we tried to eliminate our need to blossom and prosper I think that we could not. So we hurt now and then. But, while noticing the occasional pain, we can keep our eyes on doing what we need to do to achieve that success. And, in that very doing, we succeed.

Read carefully here. Constructive Living holds that a certain degree of suffering in human existence is natural, inevitable, even beneficial. Suffering doesn't have to be pleasant or desirable or endured forever. But many of the distressed people I see in teaching sessions have made a major goal of life the avoidance of discomfort. They have twisted and turned away from their life goals and their daily activities at the first sign of discomfort. They have tried to dodge anguish at all cost. They pay the price of their unnatural life-style. Hurting is part of life. We avoid the hurt that we can avoid. But we don't let the hurt move us away from Constructive Living. We use it; we suffer its existence; we keep moving toward our goals.

Pain—it's all in your mind, but it's *real.* All that you know about Reality is in your mind; pain is another part of the flow of experience which is Reality for you. It is no more imaginary than this book or the light by which you read. Given that pain is real, what can be done about it?

As I write these words, I'm suffering from the throbbing ache of a wisdom tooth that wishes to be born into a world with no room for it. The pain fades in and out of awareness as I turn my attention to this task and the next. Last night I took an aspirin in order to ease things enough to get to sleep. (If it's raining and you have an umbrella, there's no harm in using it.)

From the Constructive Living point of view there is nothing particularly terrific about suffering. There is nothing I have learned in the scientific psychological West or the mystical East which makes me enjoy hurting. On the other hand, hurting need not prevent us from getting done what needs doing in our lives. This morning I was up at 5:30 here on Kauai, in Hawaii, and into the garden, as usual. As I struggled with the weeds and raked leaves from the lawn there were moments when the pain was out of my awareness. Those moments were as pain free as though I had taken some complicated drug. There were other moments, too.

The pain reminds me to look for hypothetical causes—the shaved ice I chewed, the hard nuts I crunched with those rear molars—and to see whether careful attention to avoiding these sources could prevent further problems. Or perhaps that wisdom tooth should be extracted. Pain gets my attention. It says, "Do something about me!" Rational, logical arguments don't seem to have much affect on pain.

Pain reminds me of my limits. It points toward the limits of my tolerance for discomfort, my impatience, my mortality. It reminds me of how easy it is to get upset when all isn't going my way on my schedule. It forces me to decide about priorities. For a while after it goes away, it helps me feel grateful for its absence.

Now it just hurts.

The Zen koan about when it's hot, just be fully hot; and when it's cold, just be fully cold applies to pain, as well. There is no need to add anything to the natural suffering caused by a rambunctious wisdom tooth. There is no need to add such ruminations as: I wish I weren't hurting, if I hadn't made those mistakes perhaps I wouldn't be suffering now, I've done what I could why does the ache keep taunting me, is God punishing me for something, I suffer more than I deserve, and on and on. The mind tends to generate twiddlings of this sort to add on top of the natural pain. It takes some discipline to get on about what one is capable of doing under the circumstances, letting the mind spin away, enduring the pain while making efforts to relieve it.

Pain, pain, go away!
Come again some other day.

As with any aspect of our daily lives, we must accept the reality of pain as it is. Then we go about doing what we can to change that reality. To try to skip the step of acceptance is to open ourselves to additional, needless discomfort.

DAVID K. REYNOLDS

On Painting

For twenty years I have been painting watercolors, mostly landscapes and flowers. This endeavor is part of my personal exploration of the psychological events that comprise discovering and doing what needs to be done.

As I paint, what needs doing keeps emerging from the paper. That is, as colors and line/forms build, they suggest the need for the next line/forms and colors. The situation calls forth the next appropriate behavior. This calling forth of appropriate action is relatively straightforward in the restricted realm of painting. But the principle applies to our everyday lives. Situations suggest proper responses from us.

During the process of putting brush to paper my hand moves faster than my rational mind can follow. There is no time for full rational analysis of each stroke. There is just a general sense of what is yet incomplete, where action is necessary, and the direction the necessary action should take. Again, life brings many such events to us—events in which we have no time to plan out every small detail of our response. Our very speech follows this form. We have no time to plan out each word of each sentence as we speak. Yet word follows word in the general direction we have chosen for our talking. The words "appear" as we speak them rather like the brush strokes in my paintings "appear."

Painting, like writing, provides the occasion for losing myself in the moment's activity. Hours may pass as the pen and brush keep responding to what Reality has brought them. I can experience without rationally understanding this intense focus of attention. At times it feels as though the brush takes on a life of its own, moving as it wills. It is the same sort of transcendent sense as "grooving" in tennis or basketball or golf. The body works smoothly to accomplish the task set before it. Almost without thought, just sketching, just swinging, just shooting, just stroking.

I notice more about flower petals and leaves and stems now that I paint them. I remember more about colors and the details of shapes. The doing of painting has opened a flower window on the world. The doing has changed me.

DAVID K. REYNOLDS

Health Benefits of Constructive Living

A number of studies have shown that people are more susceptible to illness after they have encountered some stressful (positive or negative) life event such as loss of a spouse, birth of a child, marriage, loss of a job, promotion, and so forth. In a study conducted on Western subjects Kobasa (1981) found that people with characteristics of "hardiness" were less likely to become physically ill after stressful life events than people who didn't show these traits of hardiness. Kobasa's work suggests that certain traits of character minimize the impact on health of such stressful events.

What is hardiness according to this researcher? It is composed of three traits. The first is commitment, the ability to become deeply involved in a task or project. The second is control, the attitude that one can influence the world by one's actions. Such an attitude is opposite to that of hopelessness or helplessness. It appears to be what other researchers have called an internal locus of control. The third trait is challenge, the attitude that change is natural and stimulating rather than threatening.

Do such characteristics sound familiar? They are basic elements of Constructive Living. Attention to our immediate tasks, an active and positive life-style, and the acceptance of inevitable change as a part of human existence are fundamental to our Constructive Living teaching. These elements correspond to commitment, control, and challenge, as described above. A side benefit of Constructive Living seems to be better physical health in the face of the "slings and arrows of outrageous fortune."

Information and Responsibility

Recently, my watch began to malfunction. Made by a fine Japanese company, it is a very useful watch with many functions. Though the warranty period had expired, I took the watch to the company service center for repairs. In a few days the watch was returned to me by mail, fully repaired, with new batteries at no charge. Needless to say, I was quite pleased by the prompt and free service. Only one service was lacking. I would have liked to know what was wrong with the watch and whether there was something I could do to prevent the malfunction again.

Similarly, there are still too few physicians or auto mechanics who will take the time to explain what they are doing and why or what we can do to reduce the chances of further problems. Perhaps they think that their specialty is too difficult for laypersons to understand, perhaps they think that fixing the problem is all that is necessary. Can I be dissatisfied when my watch is fixed skillfully and quickly for free? Though I am grateful for the fine service, there is something yet needing to be done.

If we are to act responsibly in the world we need information. The most obviously useful information might be called "dedicated" information. It tells us what happened and what to do in certain special circumstances. It is patently practical, the kind of information contained in the manual for a video recorder or a new car. Such information could also be attached to the bill for repair service, with cause and solution and future prevention circled among a list of commonly encountered problems.

Another kind of information might be called "general." It comes from keeping our eyes open, reading widely, listening during conversations, taking general education classes, and so forth. Such information may not help prevent our clogging the garbage disposal, but it broadens us and helps us evaluate the usefulness of other information we encounter.

Then there is "theoretical" information. This information helps us understand the principles on which our world operates. It helps us organize information and connect information from different areas of our lives.

Constructive Living teaches us to hold ourselves responsible for what we do. To act responsibly we need to be informed. So we are responsible, too, for seeking information. Such responsibility doesn't go against our grain. We are a curious species (in both senses of the word "curious"). Although the knowledge base in the modern world becomes more and more intricate, specialized, and complex we need to keep up with informing ourselves. And specialists with expertise gained over long years of training and experience need to clarify and simplify information so that the informed public can keep abreast of general developments in a variety of fields.

Passion in Perspective

NEUROTIC LOVE

Just as neurotic individuals narrow their perspective to make themselves the center and prime occupant of the universe, neurotic love at its broadest fails to see beyond the boundaries of the dyad, the couple. This narrowed, self-focused perspective is classically characteristic of neurotic moments.

The man who thinks only of himself and his reflection in his lover's eyes limits his chances of success to a small field of play. The women who spend their lunch breaks talking about the men in their lives, who daydream about their future with these men, who wonder what their lovers are doing at this moment, can break free from their obsession by finding broader purposes, a lifework that goes beyond the romantic moment, interests that expand their awareness and make them better companions because of their new breadth.

Even within the dyad, neurotic love demands that one get one's own share. Taking, self-protection, monitoring the balance of power, and meeting one's own needs take priority. The joys of giving, gratitude, and service are subservient to the neurotic self-centeredness. Again, the course toward change lies in changed behavior. Giving, serving, submitting, exploring the companion's needs, thanking, apologizing, and the like are behaviors undertaken consciously, not from weakness or by default, but purposefully. At first, the goal may be to develop oneself within the context of the dyad, and then one sees that such actions are simply proper and rewarding in themselves.

OVERPLAYED EMOTIONS

I suspect that the role of emotions in everyday life is exaggerated in our times. The performing arts have brought emotional extremes before our eyes again and again. Novelists spice their works with violent emotions and actions. Song lyrics emphasize strong feelings. Bombarded by this rain of passion we find ourselves losing perspective on the normal range of emotional experience in our lives. Compared with what we see and hear on television and at the theater our emotional lives may seem pale and undramatic.

Our lives are unlikely to have the constant roller coaster ups and downs of the characters in the media. Some people seem to make efforts to live up to the images portrayed in the arts. It all seems so exciting.

Morita discouraged the reading of novels by his students, particularly during the early period of their life training. The reason offered was that neurotically suffering people try to escape into the fantasy world of novels rather than facing and acting to effect changes in their everyday lives. But I think there is another reason for the limiting of such escapes these days. Novels (as well as dramas on television, in the theater, and in films) are likely to distort the impact of emotional pressure on humans.

We need not be so pushed about by passion. We have much more control over what we do, how we behave, than would appear from shows with dramatic effect. Seeing so much of this imaginative drama, some people begin to believe that they are dominated by the same powerful feelings portrayed by actors and actresses. It isn't so. Life isn't nearly as extreme or as unstable as what we see on the stage. Who, after all, would pay to see everyday life as it really is? What sort of entertainment would that be?

Our lives are built more on doing than on feeling. Certainly, whatever stability and security exists in our lives comes from our behavior, from our steady and goal-directed behavior. Washing

DAVID K. REYNOLDS

the dishes, checking the oil level in our cars, filing the manila folder, closing the shutters, sweeping the leaves, carrying out the trash, balancing the checkbook, and the like aren't activities likely to attract people to buy tickets for the theater or paperbacks from a bookstore. But in those countless daily activities we invest much of our lives. They provide us with the opportunity to tune ourselves to reality. Along with other activities they give us the chance to find satisfaction in accomplishment on a variety of levels.

While the shifting winds of emotion whistle through our lives, we can anchor ourselves solidly by doing well what needs to be done.

On Realistic Gratitude

Gratitude is a feeling and so is uncontrollable directly by our will. We cannot generate gratitude simply by telling ourselves to be grateful. On the other hand, however, gratitude is a natural response to keeping our eyes open as we operate in the world. It takes a certain amount of effortful blindness to miss the truth of Reality's moment-by-moment support of our lives. From the oxygen we breathe to the efforts of others who provide our food and our stereos, our comfort and our education, our livelihood and our sports partners—we "are lived" by Reality.

Constructive Living holds that the realistic gratitude we experience as we take notice of the supportive nature of our world carries with it a desire to repay the world somehow and a certain degree of sadness or guilt that we aren't doing more along the lines of balancing our debts to the world.

I am not interested in arguing these points. I take them as self-evident. At this moment in time you either understand and recognize what I have written here or you don't. If you give this lifeway a serious try, you will come to insights of the sort mentioned above. Beware that you don't walk in a direction leading toward an undesired goal.

One learns about Reality (and oneself as part of Reality) by acting in it. Everyday life is our best teacher. By directing and noticing what we do in our daily lives we learn about ourselves.

By paying attention to what Reality sends our way we learn about Reality.

Some of my students talk a great deal about knowing themselves. They have invested long periods of time in analyzing their thoughts and feelings. They have great insights into their rationalizations, their psychological defenses, their coping mechanisms, their infantile fixations, and such. They need to pay more attention to what they do. In doing what is purposeful and proper to the varied situations of life, they find that they have less need for elaborate theories of the mind. They discover that much of their intellectual theorizing had been used as an escape from responsible, attentive living. They get on about paying their debts to the world.

Morita pointed out that our intellectual understanding and our feelings don't always match one another neatly. We may know that we won't smash the valuable pot we hold in our hands, but we still feel fear that we might do so. We might feel uncomfortable looking down from a height, all the while knowing that we are being very careful not to lose our balance. We may know that this particular snake or insect is harmless and yet feel revulsion and terror while handling the creature. We may realize that the celebrity in front of us is just another human but feel awed and nervous all the same. As we act in the world we learn about these conflicts and contradictions. We come to accept them as natural aspects of our psychological functioning. In the acceptance, we find they have less power over us. Because these contradictions are part of us, by accepting them we are accepting ourselves. This hang-up is just another aspect of me, and I am just another aspect of this Reality in this Moment. It's all quite natural. Now, what needs to be done next? And we get on about living.

Some of my students complain that they feel no gratitude toward work. They can find nothing interesting about working in general. They would prefer to pass their days gently in idleness. Yet they feel some vague discomfort, as though they should be feeling more productive, they should be making more of a contribution to the world. For most of us, sitting and thinking about work is no fun. The way we develop an interest in some aspect of

DAVID K. REYNOLDS

Reality, work included, is by acting on it. So we must be careful about the activities in which we engage. Our interests will follow along in the directions of our activities. As for work, our interest in some task has the opportunity to grow when we undertake the task. It is foolishness to wait for interest and gratitude toward work to grow as we sit on the couch watching television. Performing our tasks develops interest in them.

Similarly, we outgrow our narrow self-doubts and anxieties by leaving them alone as we go on about living well. We grow accustomed to our shyness and self-criticism and find such traits diminishing as we exert effort in our activities and succeed. We may even come to feel gratitude toward our neurotic past-selves because they prodded us to discover this wonderful lifeway. We become adaptable, flexible, natural, truly alive.

Thankfulness is a natural consequence of this process. As we shift from self-focus to Reality-focus we recognize what Reality is presenting to us. Our actions become purpose-filled with concrete, specific deeds of repayment. We see ourselves no longer standing apart from Reality, demanding our proper share, but as part of Reality, benefitted and benefitting others.

Pacing Ourselves

Sometimes I find myself hurriedly moving from one task to another, operating at a pace faster than is required by reality. In this world of dizzying activity it is easy to be seduced into habits of rushing about.

When I notice the beginnings of such a tendency I shift my effort to doing the same tasks with grace and aesthetic emphasis. It isn't sufficient to tell myself, "Slow down!" My mind is still moving along at a fast clip; my body tries to catch up. So I put that accelerating mind to work finding the most beautiful way to get dressed, to water the plants, to dust, to move the furniture, to change the spark plugs in the car.

Over the years, our minds learn to do many projects relatively automatically, so the free mental energy becomes nervous energy devoted to speed. The relatively unfamiliar task of finding beauty in an everyday task absorbs the excess energy and results in a natural slowing of our pace of life. And there is real satisfaction in doing a simple task tastefully.

The opposite problem of pace sometimes occurs, too. There are times when we wake up feeling sluggish, times when we are overly well rested, times when we need to pick up the pace of our actions because Reality requires it. The solution is quite predictable: Not feeling like it, we put our bodies in motion. Physical activity—whether it be exercises, jogging, a brisk walk, beating rugs, or a plunge in the pool—perks up our pace in a way that sitting on the couch daydreaming cannot.

We can use our purposes and actions in ways to regulate the march of our moments. Keeping an eye on Reality and its demands, keeping an eye on where we want to be tomorrow and next year and twenty years from now, and keeping in mind the means by which we move to achieve our goals we have the opportunity to determine the optimally shifting pace of our lives. As always, this lifeway requires effort and attention. It is well worth the investment.

PART II:

CONSTRUCTIVE LIVING
PEOPLE

In the section that follows are found accounts of Constructive Living students. Their names and details of their stories have been modified to preserve their anonymity.

Blind Spots

Some people are hurting so badly that they want to be like everyone else. They are mistaken in two ways. They think that others don't hurt, at least in the same ways and to the same extent that they do. And they think that they can become like everybody else.

They have no choice but to be different, but they have a choice in determining the direction of that difference. They have the abilities to live *superior* lives.

Nowadays, Connie can laugh at the excuses she makes for her successes. She was never one to excuse her failures. Failures seemed natural and inevitable to Connie. They were properly understood by her weakness, her faults, and her neurotic personality—or so she thought. But successes required special explanations, even excuses.

When she was able to sign her name for credit card purchases without trembling it had to be because the salesperson wasn't looking and her friend was off browsing in another part of the store. When she was praised for her fine work she believed that her manager had simply overlooked the mistakes that she must have made. When life went smoothly for awhile it was because of unusual circumstances, the efforts of others, a temporary lull in her nervousness, mistakes that slipped by unnoticed, the temporary influence of Constructive Living in her life, and so on and on. Success wasn't natural; failure was.

The tendency is still there after five sessions of Constructive Living guidance. But she *notices* it, catches herself doing it, and laughs. She has reached an important stage. It is a stage similar to that reached by Charlie.

Charlie criticizes himself unmercifully. In his daily journal he berates himself for the pep talks he uses to psyche himself into getting up, going for a run, getting to work on time, and almost every activity in which he engages. He catches himself not noticing his surroundings. He uncovers his tendency to daydream. He spots his jealousy and dissatisfaction with what he has achieved in comparison with what his peers are achieving.

What Charlie is only beginning to see is that his noticing these quirks is an important step in changing them. Before, he simply imagined his way through life, stumbling, marking time, lying where he fell. All the time he felt a sometimes vague and sometimes sharp uneasiness. Life ought to be better than the way he was living it. His self-criticism was blurred and pervasive. Now it is sharp and focused. Now it is clearer what needs to be done to change the way he lives.

I keep telling Charlie that this catching himself in sloppy living is a very positive step for him. Miyamoto Musashi, the famed Japanese swordsman, really meant it when he wrote that "The Way is in training." Training doesn't lead to or result in finding the Way to live. Training, in itself, is being on the Way. That subtle alteration in attention which allows us to catch our minds trying to con us or run along in old unconstructive habitual ruts *is* being on the Way. The same process of bringing attention back again and again to the focal breathing or mantra or counting or whatever during meditation can be applied to daily living. We examine what we attend to and get on about doing what needs doing. Such is the Way.

Charlie used to see only the painfulness of the self-criticism. Connie used to see the naturalness of her failure alone. Blind spots. Charlie wanted to eliminate the self-criticism. Connie wanted to eliminate the failure. Why not recognize the usefulness of both and learn from them? Connie can learn the naturalness of success and of change in general by expanding her attitude toward

DAVID K. REYNOLDS

the naturalness of failure. Charlie can learn that his discoveries of momentary slips mean not only failure but successful monitoring, correcting, and steps along the Way.

Failure and self-criticism aren't pleasant. They are downright painful. But they aren't "bad." They aren't best handled by wiping them out, even if we could. They teach us. They are to be used for our growth. Yes, they even deserve our thanks. Blind spots only occur in relationship to certain points of view. Looked at from another perspective a blind spot disappears. Whether it is a stop sign hidden by a willow branch or a truth hidden by pain, there is a place from which Reality can be clearly seen.

A Vast Difference

Elementary principles of thinking, feeling, living aren't taught in our schools. They aren't understood by our children. It is rather surprising, therefore, to see such a specialized technique as psychoanalysis in common use in therapy settings. It is as though therapists were trying to teach a college course to patients who never attended grammar school. It is no wonder that patients misunderstand what they are about in psychoanalysis. It is no wonder that many psychoanalysts misunderstand, too. For they, too, never learned elementary-school-level principles of the mind.

Marta doesn't yet believe that she is in something fundamentally different from the more than ten years of psychoanalysis she experienced before coming for Constructive Living training. She thinks she is engaged in some variant of analysis. She brings the same old habits of thinking and talking, the same old emphasis on feelings, the same old self-focus. The first few sessions are rather bewildering to Marta. She plays the role of obedient little girl, then she shifts to the role of critical, spiteful, "difficult" patient. At last, she gets down to business, trying the exercises, asking questions, reporting on what she did during the week.

During the period of showing me her spiteful self, Marta thought she detected that something she said had hurt me. She was rather surprised to find that I recognized and admitted to feeling hurt. She had expected a more impassive, unassailable "therapist." She was more surprised to hear that I didn't think the hurt I felt at the moment amounted to much. It passes like any other feeling. Constructive Living is not about eliminating or defending against hurt; it is about behaving constructively whether one is hurting or not. The resiliency and flexibility more than makes up for the vulnerability. To try to defend ourselves against unpleasant feelings leaves us rigid and small, and the fortification never works well anyway. When Marta hurts me, I'll hurt, but I'll continue being there for her, teaching her what I believe she needs to learn. And the hurt will pass.

Winning and Losing the Game of Life

At a recent group session, a student described the discomfort she felt trying to write clearly, without trembling, when someone was watching her write. She had come to the point of doing her writing at home to avoid the eyes of others. For her, winning the contest with her "symptom" meant being able to write calmly and well in front of others.

Her goal is misdirected and uninformed. She may never win the game that she has set up for herself. In fact, she sees that she is losing day by day. In time she learned that winning her contest lies not in writing perfectly in front of others, much less in avoiding the confrontation with herself by writing in private at home. True winning means continuing to write whenever and wherever the occasion demands, even though her hand shakes, even though she feels foolish and embarrassed. Victory is being able to fail and come back to try again and to fail and to come back once more. Over and over. When she becomes skillful at the genuine game, she is quite likely to find that she has also won the pseudo game she set up for herself.

Two Students

Readers of earlier books have asked for more detailed descriptions of individual students' experiences in Constructive Living, what would be called "case studies" in psychotherapy. Here we take a look at the learning course of a couple of Los Angeles students.

STUDENT #1

Warren H. is a handsome, blond, Caucasian male in his mid-thirties. He works as a movie-studio cameraman. He lives by the beach.

Warren has a history of drug abuse, although he has been free of drugs for several years. He pulled himself out of the drug scene with special diets, exercise, and meditation. Warren came to the ToDo Institute with complaints of depression in response to the final stages of his forthcoming divorce. He had had some contact with meditation in the Zen style and had read about Morita therapy in a Zen Center newspaper. He believed that this form of therapy would fit his current life-style aiming at self-improvement.

First Session

In the first one-hour session I obtained a brief history and asked him about his understanding of Constructive Living. I asked about his previous experience in therapy. I inquired about what brought him to this setting at this time and what he expected to gain from therapy here.

After about thirty minutes I asked Warren to close his eyes and to describe the room without looking. He had noted very little about the room's details although he could tell me about major furnishings and the color of my shirt. This simple test helped me determine how much of his attention was reserved for inner psychological functioning and how much was free for focus on the external world. Warren was not totally caught up in his suffering.

I assigned Warren the task of attending fully to the details of everyday life. He was to notice which foot hit the floor first as he got out of bed in the morning, how he turned on the water faucet, the order in which he soaped his body in the shower, and so forth. I also asked him to buy and read two books: *Playing Ball on Running Water* and *Constructive Living*. These books were written to help him understand the principles of the lifeway he would be learning.

Warren was told when he first telephoned for an appointment that I would be in Japan for about five weeks. He wanted to begin his study right away, nevertheless. We planned to continue our work together upon my return. In the meantime, he was to work on his assignments and to see a physician for a physical examination.

The week after my return from Japan Warren called the ToDo Institute office and stated his desire to continue the training. We made a second appointment.

Second Session

At the second session Warren said that he had enjoyed reading the books and had recommended them to several friends. He pointed out that after reading them he was aware of some of the problems he and his friends had in viewing the world, so he could see how these books might be helpful in straightening out difficulties in their lives.

Warren noted that his focused attention on everyday activities was quite interesting at first, but in a few days he began to forget to do the exercise. He noted that much of his life had been like that—initial interest then not following through. He realized that it would do no good to make noble and detailed plans in his life if he had no habit of carrying out his plans.

He asked an intellectual and theoretical question about how we determine what needs to be done. I brought him back from the intellectual level to the immediate, concrete, here-now reality. He asked about the value of planning the next day's activities on the night before. I recommended that if he were to plan in such detail, that he write down his plans. I explained that I would try to re-direct all his cognitive effort into physical action. I suspected that he wouldn't take the trouble to write down minute plans for the following day. Reality seldom allows us to carry out detailed plans of a day's activities anyway. Rather than perfect organization, we are aiming at proper response to what reality brings us moment by moment, I explained.

Warren recognized his tendency to turn much of life into intellectual, theoretical discussion.

I assigned the Constructive Living journal. A sheet of paper was divided vertically into two columns. On one side was to be written what he was doing at a particular point in time. On the other side was to be written what he was thinking and feeling at that point in time. I pointed out some of the purposes of the diary: 1) to get a sense of the changing flow of feelings, 2) to see that there is no necessary fit between what one feels and does at a point in time, 3) to give him practice dividing his experience into what is controllable directly (behavior) and what is not (feelings). I also warned him not to write in the journal on the feelings side in detail and neglect the behavior side. I wanted as much detail on the one side of each page as on the other. He was to write a page a day (any time period would be all right—6:05 P.M., 6:12 P.M., 6:32 P.M., and if a page was filled, that would be sufficient for the day; or 7:15 A.M., 12:30 P.M., 4:45 P.M., 8:52 P.M. would be acceptable, as well).

He was also instructed to continue with his attention to the details of everyday life. When questioned, he couldn't tell me which shirt sleeve he put on first that morning or many details of his day (who he passed as he was running, which shoe went on first, differences in plants and buildings he regularly walked past, and so forth).

I gave him a brief preview of what was to come in the training after he gained more mastery over the attention to everyday life. He was interested in grand purposes. I mentioned the Naikan exercises of reflection on what was received from and given to others, the troubles we cause them, the debt we owe to our world. But we agreed that Warren was not yet ready for such exercises. At this point he would just listen to their description, agree that they are probably valuable, and do nothing about them concretely. Warren needed to make his behavior base more solidly grounded at this time.

We agreed to meet one week later. But Warren made no further appointments.

STUDENT #2

First Session *(weekly sessions, one hour each)*

Judy was an attractive, slim, thirty-nine-year-old Caucasian divorced woman living with Ronald, a painter, and former husband of a well-known singer. His son, Jeremy, lives with Judy and Ronald most of the time because the child's mother is busy and takes little responsibility for the child. Judy came for study because she had become unhappy in the relationship. Ronald spent little time with her, focusing on his work. He believed Judy hadn't accepted and mothered Jeremy as he expected her to do. According to Judy, he increasingly saw her as a sort of burdensome demand on his time and attention. Several times he had talked of breaking up, but she always begged him to stay, and he did.

Judy saw herself as giving up more and more for Ronald. She used to meditate. She used to see more of her sister. Now most of her life and thinking was focused on Ronald. She worked as a middle-level executive in a business setting. At work she had been promoted to a new position where her superior was unorganized. She had less decision-making power than she would have liked at work.

Second Session

At the end of this session Judy wrote down the following assignments: Write the business reports due at work, go to a party with Ronald, write in the daily journal for a week, finish reading a book about Morita therapy, attend a museum exhibit, do grocery shopping, do laundry.

My notes for this session end with the reminder to talk more about what needs doing with Ronald.

Third Session

Judy was slightly tearful at the beginning of this session. I handed her a box of tissue. She reported that she and Ronald had decided to break up. They were both looking for separate apartments although they would continue to live together until new living arrangements were made. Jeremy would be with his mother for a few months. This separation and a couple of upcoming painting commissions for Ronald had prompted the timing of this breakup. Judy noted that the separation was initiated by Ronald. But this time Judy didn't beg him to stay.

She felt lost and abandoned. She did spend some time with her sister and with her parents. She felt loved and supported by them. She could lean on them. It even appeared that her sister felt closer to Judy now that Judy allowed her to be supportive.

Judy had interesting assumptions about her situation. She seemed to believe that going through hell during a breakup "validated" the relationship as having been deep and pure. She was appalled that Ronald seemed to be taking everything so well—he could sleep well, for example. Another assumption was that talking things out would result in their reconciling and would allow Ronald the chance to express the feelings that he "must" be bottling up inside.

We discussed the difference between the single-focused love of many women and the more diffuse focus of many men. These foci are, in part, reinforced by the topics of conversation of the sexes and by their activities. Judy didn't have to consider herself devalued by Ronald's lack of upset over the breakup.

Judy's image of herself didn't need to be built on the mirror of Ronald's eyes. Those who are so dependent on others' evaluations have little confidence in their own ability to react properly with constructive behavior in upsetting situations. It is important to build life on our own deeds. Judy had been in many therapies where she had examined the sources of her weakness and her dependence on others' evaluations for a sense of self-worth. Knowing the sources (and I doubt that her recollections of the past were any more accurate than those of anyone else) didn't help eliminate the tendency.

I pointed out that as we talked about preparations for finding an apartment and other practical matters and as she described the meals with her family her face changed, her tears disappeared, the pain of the separation disappeared temporarily. We discussed the story of two women who had broken up with their respective lovers at about the same time. One continually reminded herself about the breakup by listening to records and reading letters from her former lover. The other went about putting reminders of her man behind her. Finding a new place to live and putting aside unnecessary reminders of Ronald would help reduce the ruminating about the past and help Judy get on with life in the present. Of course, she could expect to think of Ronald now and again. But natural recollections and making efforts to keep him in mind are quite different matters.

Even during this crisis period, Judy had recognized her ability to continue to notice her surroundings and to go on about life's business without falling apart. She noted the relief she felt going to the structured work situation on weekdays and the particular difficulties of less active weekends. I quizzed her about the morning's events in detail. She had noticed even small details. She was pleased at her ability to do so. I praised her for continuing to attend to Reality even during these trying times.

She remarked, "I know what you are saying is right. But, of course, it is the doing that is important." She realized that it is easy to find these ideas intellectually attractive in good times, but it is hard to remember to act constructively in times of upset. Then she began to think that the ideas of Constructive Living were all right for some people, but not for her. However, Judy was coming to see that she was able to act on these principles and, when she did so, she found benefit in them. She compared her current breakup with one in her twenties when she did nothing for months afterward. Already, in the midst of her life turmoil she had found a job opening for a better position and had applied for it.

I reminded her that I was teaching her to play a life game that could be won consistently. The outcomes don't necessarily turn out as we expect or hope, but the doing of our lives well generates character. The assignments aimed at helping her exhibit strength in time of trouble. The aim was to build character, not to eliminate her suffering. The indirect result of character growth would be reduced suffering, however.

At this time her assignments were to continue her daily journal, to serve Ronald, and consider his convenience (not for any sexist reasons, but because this might be her final chance to give to this human) until the final separation. For example, she was not to keep him up late at night trying to talk it out when he wanted to go to sleep, as she had in the past. Judy was to notice and resist her tendency to try to turn this service into a way to keep Ronald in the relationship with the notion that if she served him well he might decide to stay. The service was to be carried out because she needed to do it, because she didn't want to feel guilt about what she could have done, but didn't do, for him during their last days together. In addition, she was instructed to find out about the problems faced by her sister and parents and to support them. She was to do her work diligently without complaining or seeking excessive support from fellow workers, to continue searching for an apartment, to continue her regular program of running exercise, and to write a letter of farewell to Jeremy to be delivered on his return.

Fourth Session

Judy remarked that she got through the week surprisingly well, compared with the breakups she experienced in the past. She had taken several meals with her family, found an apartment, continued to run, slept and ate well. She had gone to work regularly.

There were times when her mind drifted off at work, times when she slept fitfully, times when she wanted more attention and response from Ronald. But, on the whole, the week had gone well.

She wrote in her journal regularly and listened to her family members' problems. However, she still hadn't written the letter to Jeremy. She felt guilt toward Jeremy for not feeling as much love and affection toward him as Ronald wanted. We talked about the impossibility of generating feelings to order. What had she done for Jeremy? We moved from talking about uncontrollable feelings to controllable behavior. She talked about ignoring some of his wishes and requests. She felt great resentment toward the child for interfering with her private time with Ronald. She believed that writing a letter and giving a parting gift to Jeremy would validate Ronald's assessment that she hadn't given enough of herself to the child when they were together.

I asked her to recount in detail a period of several hours from the past week. She selected the previous night and described her behavior in some, but not much, detail. She asked whether the training would continue on this "surface" level. She wanted deeper, more difficult assignments. I told her that she was moving through a crisis period in her life. I was pleased that she had so much interest and energy to ask for more to do. So I gave her a menu of assignments and asked her to select from among them what she would do during the following week. I suggested three books for reading (*If You Meet the Buddha on the Road, Kill Him!, Naikan Psychotherapy,* and *The Quiet Therapies*), reflecting on what others had done for her during the day, followed by writing a page on specific reflections, and thanking objects (silently, to herself) for their service.

I inquired if she would like to skip the next session and begin again after my return from Hawaii, a period of about six weeks. She wished to meet once more before my departure. I gave her my telephone number and address in Hawaii, as is customary.

Fifth Session

Judy's sister's friend, Ellen, began Constructive Living guidance this week. Judy had recommended the Constructive Living guide and books to Ellen.

Judy appeared well and in control of her behavior. During the session she was briefly tearful at times when talking about Ronald and her loneliness. We noted that her feelings fluctuated with the topic of our conversation, that she smiled when discussing work.

Judy believed she had exhausted her sister with her complaints and sorrows. Her sister now seemed to be busy when Judy wanted to get together with her. At work there was a woman who inquired about Judy's problems and offered sympathy. I suggested that Judy stop talking about her difficulties with this lady. Judy asked how she could handle questions like, "How are you doing today, Honey?" Perhaps a deflection like, "Pretty well. How about you?" would suffice.

I repeated the earlier recommendation that Judy get interested in finding out about and being helpful to other people, even though she hasn't fully recovered from the separation from Ronald. I brought up the possibility that I might appear cold and unfeeling in making such suggestions, but that my genuine purpose was to guide Judy to a strategy that would work to relieve much of her unnecessary suffering. She seemed to understand. In fact, already she was remarking that she could predict what I was likely to say in response to her questions. We began looking at termination of her Constructive Living study, followed by sessions only when she considered them necessary.

Judy hadn't seen Ronald in three weeks. Sometimes she wondered what he was doing, with whom he was going out. His commission work had been completed a month earlier so that it was no longer a matter of his job keeping them apart. They had talked recently by phone; he said that he wanted space. She saw more clearly now that, for him, their relationship was ended. She still had some vague desire to confront him, talk it out, and win him back to her. Yet she knew that to attempt such a course would be futile.

Her new apartment was properly furnished at this time. She attended concerts and classes, but she disliked coming home to an empty place. She had had no dates with other men yet.

There were many applicants for the new position she had desired; she didn't get as far as an interview. But her current job held steady. She continued to eat well and to run regularly. She occasionally had trouble sleeping.

She recognized the benefits she had obtained from Constructive Living guidance, particularly when comparing her life now with her life after an earlier breakup. At the end of the session I asked her to close her eyes and to describe the room in detail. She was able to do so, incorporating information that was recent and different. We were both pleased with her success. She said that she didn't observe consciously; it had begun to be a habit, incorporated in her daily life. It was one more indication that she had the energy and attention free to notice and act in the real world.

Her final assignments included a note of gratitude and gift to her sister, refraining from complaints and discussion of Ronald with others, and continuing to live actively.

PART III:

MAXIMS, KOANS, AND EXERCISES

Some of the regular teaching methods of Constructive Living are included in this section. Use them to deepen your understanding of this lifeway.

Maxims

HONOR YOUR DENTAL FLOSS

Dental floss gets used and thrown away without a thought. How is it different from your toothbrush? Why do you reuse your toothbrush and throw away dental floss? The smallest, cheapest of objects serve us every day. They deserve our attention, proper use (or reuse), and thanks. It isn't foolish to thank your dental floss.

LIFE MAY UNRAVEL BUT DON'T LOSE THE THREAD

We may forget the principles of Constructive Living for a period of time, and we may "wake up" to discover we have slipped back into a feeling-centered life-style. When that happens we simply pick up the thread and begin knitting away at life again.

CLEAN SPEECH

It is helpful to get rid of sloppy and inaccurate habits of speech that only serve to perpetuate misunderstandings and "misemphases." Examples of phrases that should be avoided (with preferred phrases in parentheses) are: "If you feel like it" (If that needs doing); "I feel that" (I think that or I believe that); "How are you feeling?" (How are you doing? or How are things going?); "Enjoy your day!" (Do what needs doing!); "We're excited by your visit!" (Welcome!).

Much, not all, of what people say about feelings can be rephrased along more accurate and worthwhile lines. "Please be patient!" We don't need to be patient; we only need to wait. Patience is a feeling, hence uncontrollable. Waiting is a kind of action. Sometimes life requires that we wait. We may wait impatiently. If we busy ourselves with other tasks while waiting, we sometimes forget our impatience.

Koans

Our purpose in using these koan puzzles is not the Zen purpose of achieving enlightenment (whatever that might be), but the deepening of our understanding of Constructive Living principles.

FIREWOOD, ASHES

Firewood never becomes ashes.

At the First International Morita Counseling Seminar in Tokyo I assigned the koan, "Firewood never becomes ashes." It is a useful exercise for understanding the Constructive Living approach to living well in the present.

Koans with similar meaning include "Fear never turns into confidence," "Neurotic people never become cured," "Effort doesn't lead to peace of mind," and "My childhood, adulthood, and old age are unrelated."

I invited the seminar participants to discover the four-word solution to the firewood-ashes koan. Pithy responses can be generated for the other koans, as well.

PURPOSES

Where do purposes come from?

I recommend that my students search for the origin of their purposes. They are to trace back a purpose to the first glimmering of its appearance in their awareness. Similar koans lead them to search for the origins of anger, desires, thoughts, decisions, and other phenomena of their psyches. Try to "catch" one of these before it is full-blown in your awareness. From what does it emerge?

REALITY'S DUST

Who vacuums Reality's dust?

This koan asks the student to consider what is meant by "Reality's dust" and what is meant by the verb "to vacuum" and who does the vacuuming. If these questions are properly answered, can you answer the question, "Where does the vacuum cleaner store Reality's dust?"

BRIDGING DEATH'S CHASM

The bridge of Constructive Living crosses death's chasm.

How? No one escapes death, it seems. What can this baffling statement mean?

CALIFORNIA LOTTERY

A classmate dreamed of winning the California Lottery. He collected his prize. When he awakened he discovered that he held the winning ticket to the California Lottery. After collecting his prize, he recalled the previous night's dream. When he awakened from his reverie he felt confused. How many Lottery tickets did he buy?

Furthermore, how many times did he win the Lottery? Do you dream of success? Peace of mind? Winning lotteries?

SMOG AND SUNSHINE

Smog rolls across the land unevenly; sunshine filters brightly through the smog. The ocean breeze stirs the sunshine, ignores the smog.

What is "smog"? What causes it to roll across the land unevenly? What "sunshine" can be seen brightly through the smog? What patches of land are most highly illuminated by the sunshine—those patches without smog? Why does the ocean breeze selectively affect sunshine and smog?

Exercises

SILENCE

When practicing silence, put a coin or business card between your lips to remind yourself of your intention to limit speaking for a period of time.

TEST THE IMPOSSIBLE

Stand with right shoulder and right foot against a wall, lift your left foot and try to maintain your balance. Impossible! Stand with your heels and back against a wall, lean over and try to touch your toes while maintaining your balance. Again, impossible! So is trying to control your feelings directly by your will. So is trying to feel happy all the time. So is trying to escape from the natural and inevitable suffering of human existence. Impossible!

COMPUTE YOUR DEBTS

Compute the amount of money your father (and/or mother) has given you in cash, gifts, food, housing, and so forth: 1) since you were eighteen years old, 2) since you were born. Then compute the corresponding amount of money you have given your parents (or parent surrogates) during these same periods of time. Do the totals balance?

NINJA SILENCE

An exercise borrowed from *ninja* training is to select five-minute periods several times a day and try to carry out all activities as silently as possible. Walking, opening a loaf of bread, returning one's fork to the plate, closing the door—all done silently. The ninja were members of Japanese secret societies trained in arts of stealth. For them, this exercise was discipline for survival. The exercise sensitizes us to the ordinary clatter of our lives.

SUFI IMMOBILITY

An exercise borrowed from the *sufis* is to have the guide call "Halt!" and the student freeze until permitted to move again. (See Shah, 1964, p. 338.)

DELIBERATE DISABILITY

Try carrying out familiar tasks such as showering, dishwashing, and dressing with your eyes closed or with one hand. This exercise forces attention to the task at hand, a task that may have been carried out "automatically" in the past. You may discover other possibilities for efficient, aesthetic action as well as gratitude and appreciation of your own abilities.

A similar exercise involves using your left hand (if you are right-handed) for eating, dressing, writing, and so forth.

These exercises pull attention away from the suffering self into action made more difficult by the self-imposed limitations.

AN EXTRA HOUR

If you were given an extra hour each day, how would you spend it? What would you do with the extra hour today?

These questions are ways of getting at purposes, goals, at what is important (but, perhaps, neglected) in your life. As you become skillful at Constructive Living, you may find that blocks of time are freed up for use as you see fit. As you move smoothly from one task to the next much of the busywork of life will be done more efficiently, taking less time.

DAVID K. REYNOLDS

It is not too early to begin planning how to use your new leisure time effectively.

USING MACHINES

There is nothing unnatural about machines. They are part of our reality. There is nothing inherently wonderful about a primitive peasant existence with minimal help from machines.

Because machines are part of our everyday lives, it is best to use them productively to accomplish our goals. I find it much easier to put together these words on a word processor rather than using pencil and paper, for example. But we need not always use the machines as their designers intended. Use your imagination to create novel and constructive uses for the machinery that surrounds you.

I sometimes sit for short periods before my television watching programs recorded on my video recorder. I watch the programs at fast-scan speed. How much can I pick up without sound while everything is moving along at fifteen times its ordinary speed? It is a pleasant diversion that trains my eyes for noticing, noticing, noticing.

It is hard to do such speeded-up watching for more than five or ten minutes at a time. I begin to feel tense at that pace. So it is important to sit in a comfortable chair in as relaxed and comfortable a posture as possible. As always, what we do affects how we feel.

EXERCISE FOR NEW PARENTS

A baby, especially one's first baby, brings a flood of conflicting emotions. The responsibility, the love, the hopes, the frustrations, the exhaustion, the joy all come mixed up together. I ask a new parent to bring a photo of the baby. While looking at the photo I ask the new father or mother to make a list of what he or she wants to give the baby over the years. Then I ask the new parents to write what they must do to make these desires for their children into reality.

For example, if they want to instill a sense of honesty and trust in the child, what must they do (even today) to start those lessons.

If they want to give the child some economic security and a good education, what needs to be done (even today) to get started on achieving that goal.

These exercises may call up gratitude for our own parents' sacrifices in our behalf. Or they may call up anger at what we didn't get as children. We want the best for our children whether we received the best or not. If our parents gave us what we needed then we know and appreciate the benefits of those deeds/gifts. If our parents didn't give us what we needed then we know how much our children need those very deeds/gifts. In either case, we have learned important lessons about what we need to do for the smiling face in the photograph, the one who depends upon us.

PART IV:

CONSTRUCTIVE LIVING
CAPSULES

So many people long for the magic pill—the tranquilizer, the mantra, the get-rich scheme, the way to beat the odds in some area of life. The capsules offered here are not magic. They are no more than brief topics for reflection and discussion.

Thoughts for Constructive Living

• It isn't necessary to write a whole book at once. Just write a sentence at a time.

No journey—only steps. We invent the journey. Only the steps are real.

• Today I wrote, greeted a student, cooked dinner, played tennis. Am I a writer, a teacher, a cook, a tennis player?

Some people seem to think that I am primarily a writer or a teacher. They are wrong. Why?

• I am just a window opened to Reality. Someday the window will close. Opened or closed, Reality goes on. What is important? What is lasting?

• Reality is the guru.

Reality teaches us about which lifeways are reasonable. It teaches us about what is possible and what is impossible in our everyday lives. It relieves me of the responsibility of having to be some sort of master model for others.

Morita was asked whether, when we become upset, we should let it all hang out, angrily letting others know what is bothering us. Morita asked his questioner to reflect on past Reality. What were the results of his shouting and saying what was in his mind over the past twenty years or so? If others didn't react to his outbursts it would be hard to believe. If others did react, but he paid no attention to the results of his actions, then Morita's instruction now would be unlikely to have any effect.

Once more, Morita pointed to the teaching ability of Reality . . . when we are receptive to the teaching. Bright, sensitive people may want abstract teachings and rules from their teachers. Reality provides concrete, detailed lessons, moment by moment. Reality is the superior teacher, by far.

Instead of memorizing rules about dealing with others, it is better to examine the purposes for our own behavior and to understand the reasons underlying social rules.

• Reality sets the limits.

If you can find a method to keep you happy without any harmful side effects, let me know. If you can control your feelings by your will, thus producing joy, peace of mind, and the elimination of anger, loneliness, awkward desires with no harmful side effects, let me know.

I can't. No one I know can. Reality requires that we fit ourselves to its changes, its imposed limits, its marvelous possibilities.

• Pizza-dough mind.

A pizza-dough mind stretches to fit the changing shapes of reality. It adjusts, adapts, accepts.

• How often we look, but don't see, listen, but don't hear.

There is more to seeing than keeping our eyes open. There is a quality of receptive attention necessary for true seeing. Preconceptions and prejudices channel and block some of the information we receive from the world. So do distraction and laziness. Reality is inherently interesting. If it doesn't seem so to you, then you are not seeing and hearing.

• Somewhere along the way you have to sleep alone.

We can appreciate the companionship and support of others. Nevertheless, we are in this world on our own. No one can save me. No one can rescue me. No one can straighten out my behavior and thinking for me. I do it or I don't.

• Refine yourself through marriage.

One of the advantages of marriage or any long-term joint living arrangement is the possibility of refining our response to situations that occur again and again. As adults we begin to see how a sharp retort or a tossed-off reply affects our mate. Living together over a span of time provides us with the opportunity to try different responses to standard situations and see what reality brings us as a consequence.

• Sex is a shared pursuit.

I am told that Milton Erickson assigned couples with sexual difficulties the tasks of cooking and housecleaning together. By sharing these tasks they learned the rhythm of cooperation. Their shared cooperative spirit often extended to the bedroom, as well.

• When a house is filled with rights, there is no room for gifts.

We seem to be moving in the direction of making all matters legal and medical. What I can demand from others as my right, they cannot give me as a true gift. I am protected; yet we both lose. The medical malpractice insurance dilemma and our drug disaster are characteristic failures of our foolish attempts to solve human problems solely with external rules and medico-legal enforcement of them. We must bring about fundamental changes of the heart in order to achieve lasting solutions to our social problems.

Constructive Living Wisdom

Here are some selections concerning Constructive Living principles which I have translated, edited, and interpreted from recent issues of the Japanese Moritist magazine, *Seikatsu no Hakken (The Discovery of Life)*. The numbers following each item indicate the year, issue number, and page number of the citation.

I. FROM MORITA HIMSELF

• People want good fortune, but that isn't simply a life of ease. Feeling good isn't good fortune. Good fortune is the expression of basic character; it is effort; it springs naturally from recognizing and accepting basic desires. 86–1–43

It is likely that everyone wants good fortune in their lives. In my suicide research I came across more than a few people who lived what might be called fortunate lives, yet they killed themselves. Good fortune must be more than luck or economic success. It has something to do with a particular attitude toward life and the behavior that accompanies it.

• Be as children, handle what comes up as it comes up. 86–1–44

Anticipatory anxiety causes us unnecessary suffering. "Sufficient unto the day is the evil thereof," says the New Testament. Again, there is an appropriate time and place for planning, but as life simplifies, becomes more straightforward, we learn to respond to Reality's events as they emerge. We no longer have our minds in the office as we drive to (or from) work.

• If you think that what you are about to clean today will only be dirty again tomorrow, you'll never get anything done. Today's work today. 86-1-44

When I return from several months in Japan, there is a pile of correspondence waiting in Los Angeles. I cannot answer that pile of correspondence; it is overwhelming. It is possible, however, to answer one letter, then the next letter, and so on. Sometimes those replies will lead to further exchanges, correspondence that will continue for years. Again, the vision is intimidating. Only this letter, now.

• If we deny, suppress, or pressure the natural workings of the human mind, we interfere with the natural mind/body functions. 86-1-45

"The natural workings of the human mind." What did Morita mean by that phrase? Primarily, he meant being afraid when we are afraid, being worried when we are worried, being joyful when we are joyful, being interested when we are interested, and bored when we are bored, and so on. He advised allowing the feeling aspect of our mind/body to go its peculiar, idiosyncratic way. All the while, however, we must keep reins on the behavior aspect of our mind/body, for therein lies our personal and social responsibility. And therein lies our modicum of control over ourselves and our world (the two being aspects of the same thing, just as mind and body are aspects of the same thing).

• Enlightenment is the natural response to the environment. 86-1-46

There is no need to insert, "Now I'm on the right track" or "I must get it together, then I'll make my move" or "What does Constructive Living have to say about this situation?" To insert these glosses on Reality backs us away from enlightenment. Paying attention and responding naturally, harmoniously to what Reality presents is necessary and sufficient.

• If you worry about shyness, sweat. 86-1-49

This advice is most useful to the shy person. It is far superior to any misguided attempts to erase the shyness. It defines a life game that can be won, naturally, in the course of being shy. Sweating usually comes easily, automatically, when the shy person is in a socially tense situation. While sweating, the person can find equally natural routes for learning about others at the social event, for expressing gratitude to the host or hostess, for serving others, and the like. All these activities are natural, too.

It is common to see my students' eyes widen and smiles appear when they first hear this advice. There is also a noticeable momentary relaxation. Naturally.

• There is no need to make abstract generalizations about good and bad. The careful, detailed observation of one's functioning mind is enough. 86–4–45

I used to wonder about Morita's thinking on this subject. Then I did Naikan introspection in Japan. During Naikan we reflect on what we have received from others, what we have done in return to others, and the troubles and difficulties we have caused others. No one told us how to carve up our memories into these three categories. No one gave us absolute standards to define our good and bad behaviors and attitudes. Nevertheless, each person who seriously reflects on the past finds a set of personal standards against which past behaviors are measured. The standards evolve as the self-reflection continues. There is no need to codify my standards of right and wrong for anyone else. My proper task is to keep a mental eye on the ways my mind tries to temporarily justify and cover up my "evil" (you may prefer such words as "dysfunctional," "improper," or "inappropriate") behavior, make efforts to correct the wrong I have done, and improve my current behavior.

The "judgment seat" of my own standards allows no escape into quibbling with some externally imposed commandments. No one seems to fare very well when put up against his or her own evaluations of right and wrong during Naikan. That's interesting. Now, what do I need to do next?

• No one likes to be laughed at; no one likes to lose. Everyone wants to be great. Such is the natural condition of the human heart. 86–4–45

Was Morita merely making a trite observation here? Why do

we need to be reminded of these truths? Because we forget. We chide ourselves and others for exhibiting these characteristics. We try to teach our children that losing doesn't matter. We laugh at our dreams of greatness. We keep on being who we are.

• Death is fearsome, whatever people say about wanting to die. Desires cannot be erased, no matter how we try. 86—4—45

There is resignation and hope in these words. Morita held that there is a basic bio-psychological abhorrence of death in humans. Hold your breath to feel the beginning panic of facing breathlessness. We may be able to temporarily erase this fear with faith or philosophy, but the fear will appear from time to time.

Similarly, we may find temporary relief from awareness of our desires by distracting ourselves in one way or another. However, the desires will emerge again and again because they are fundamental, natural aspects of our biological, psychological, and social selves. We cannot erase them. Some people have written that the aim of Buddhism is to eliminate desires. I don't think so. Such a goal is impossible. One goal of Buddhism, like that of Constructive Living, is to eliminate the dominance that certain desires have over our lives.

The desire to serve others, to develop our full potential, to repay the world, and to live well in this moment are as natural as the desires to get ahead at the expense of others, to beat a rival, and to flee when embarrassed. Desires of all sorts are inevitable, inescapable. The hope lies in our ability to choose our actions, our behavior. Being angry we can accept the anger while holding back the blow, being fearful of death we can die with full attention, doing what needs doing right to the end. What may appear at first blush to be a minor field of human potential turns out to be all that we need. In fact, Reality-guided behavior permits the finest flowering of our humanity.

In the last sentence I didn't write "Self-guided behavior" because that phrase, though the same as "Reality-guided behavior," may be misinterpreted more easily. Furthermore, I did not use the words "triumph" or "victory," preferring the term "flowering" because there is no contest with Reality involved, no loser in the Constructive Life. There is cooperation, harmony, a melding with Reality.

• In feelings it is best to be wealthy and generous, i.e., to experience many feelings, to throw away many feelings. 86—6—79

Some people seem to be afraid of feelings. They try to negotiate their life paths to avoid all but the familiar and comfortable feelings. They sacrifice many useful life experiences in their attempts to keep disturbing feelings at a distance. We have a better perspective on feelings and the limits of their influence on us by welcoming them and keeping on about our purposes.

• There is no need to try to create interests and hobbies artificially. Where the eye falls, there interest is generated. 86–6–79

When students of Constructive Living realize that their lives are narrower than necessary they may desire to make a conscious effort to be involved in previously unexplored areas and pastimes. But how to go about it? How can they get started on a new hobby they know nothing about? What sort of life-enriching hobby would be best for them? Morita suggested that they begin by looking around them. By observing what is already at hand, they generate a natural curiousity to know more about their world.

I might add that, as a wider sphere of constructive action brings the eye in contact with a variety of phenomena, then the chance for the eye to fall on something interesting increases. 86–6–79

• True religion and proper tradition don't ask you to do something for the purpose of something else. If behavior springs from the pure, natural mind, it is good in itself. 86–6–82

Here is Morita's moral teaching in a nutshell. It implies a deep trust in the pure, natural mind. Behavior that springs from such a mind is good, whether or not it conforms to some externally imposed moral system. But what is the pure, natural mind? Do you expect me to tell you? Could I tell you? Look to the teacher called Reality. Reality can teach you about the pure, natural mind if you are willing and ready to learn.

• Neither changes in the body produce feelings nor do feelings produce changes in the body. Both body changes and feelings are expressions of the same phenomenon. 85–9–32

Some Western psychophysiologists have argued that sadness generates tears, others that tears generate sadness, others that they interact somehow. Some Western psychologists hold that fear produces flight; others that running away produces fear; others that fleeing and fear interact somehow. Morita, shortly after the turn of this century, held that fleeing and fright are two sides of the same coin, two ways of describing the same thing. His was, and remains, a revolutionary way of looking at feeling/doing.

Morita saw diarrhea, vomiting, and palpitations from anxiety not as symptoms of some illness called anxiety, but as further expressions of the anxiety itself. Blushing, too, he considered to be a natural expression of embarrassment. He refused to adopt the dualistic notion that physiological changes were different from psychological events. 86—1—50

II. FROM OTHER MORITISTS

In the following selections, gleaned from recent issues of the magazine, *Seikatsu no Hakken*, we can find more recent Moritist expressions of Constructive Living principles.

• Behavior makes habits; habits make character; character makes fate. 85—3—50

Change in character begins with moment-by-moment changes in behavior. Changed character brings with it a new future. There is no need to "fix" feelings and attitudes first. The first step is what we do right now.

• Notice that retreat to isolation doesn't relieve the shy person's fear of meeting other people. Behind shyness is the desire to be thought well of, to be recognized. Such desires can't be satisfied by isolation. The attempts to get rid of trembling and to feel at ease around others are side goals that aren't to the point. 84—2—16,17

We can reduce stress by avoiding meeting with other people. But stress reduction is not always appropriate for achieving our long-term goals. Keeping the stress level in our lives low is not what makes life satisfying.

• Just a moment! Wait before reacting to anxiety, to barriers. 86—1—34

We mustn't let anxiety or other upsetting feelings push us into rash action. The anxiety is natural, but it isn't a god who deserves

DAVID K. REYNOLDS

to be appeased by any sacrifice. We may need to take a few moments to look over a situation before responding to it. The delay often takes the edge off the anxiety. We may find new ways to circumvent the barrier that presents itself to us.

• Service to others produces self-gain. Altruism has self-growth value. 86–6–25

This truth is pretty much common knowledge these days. With the intellect we can divide actions into those that are for our own gain and those that are for others' gain. But, in reality, the distinctions are blurred. Some self-growth games have prospered by emphasizing the point that time invested in ourselves makes us better prepared to serve others. Constructive Living emphasizes the opposite point: Time invested in others results in self-gain.

When we invest ourselves in ourselves there is no guarantee that the results will spill over to the benefit of others. Too many of the suffering people who come for guidance have been looking out for number one. Service to others automatically and invariably produces self-gain. There may be discomfort and exhaustion. There may be lack of recognition for the service, or lack of gratitude from the recipient. But the giving away of ourselves *is* the gain itself.

• The person for whom Morita therapy was originally designed is introspective, intellectualizing, sensitive, self-conscious, persistent, socially hyperperceptive, a worrier with strong desires. 85–9–38,42

We all have some of these characteristics some of the time. Constructive Living, combining the principles of Morita therapy and Naikan, guides us toward acceptance and proper use of these qualities. There is no need to try to get rid of them.

• No one can give a perfect 100-percent effort 100 percent of the time. 85–6–43

Too often we demand perfection from ourselves and from others. Perfection isn't realistic; it isn't possible. It is a construct, a template we create in our minds. The real world has only roses, not perfect roses, just these roses.

• If you are in Tokyo and you want to go to Osaka, but you board a train heading toward the north (toward Hokkaido), no matter how long you ride the train you won't arrive in Osaka. 85–11–24

Having a goal is important. But equally important is having a realistic means of achieving that goal. No one expects to be able to board a train in Tokyo and travel to Los Angeles. Getting from Tokyo to Osaka by train is possible, if you are on the right train on the right track at the right time. Pick a lifeway that will get you where you want to go, where it's possible to go.

• No great joy comes with a genuine cure of neurosis or correction of an unproductive life-style. We simply begin doing what normally ought to be done. 85–11–26

Constructive Living merely gives us the opportunity to do what we ought to be doing, the opportunity to be ordinary, natural. That may not be enough for some people. They long for transcendant meanings and marvels. I recommend getting accustomed to riding the local train before searching around for an express.

• Anxiety is like a caution light, signaling attention to something important. 85–11–26

Anxiety warns us to take notice of something that needs our attention. We act on some problems in our environment and the anxiety goes away. Anxiety may signal the need for a visit to a professional. It may point to a biochemical disorder that requires medication.

Constructive Living does *not* recommend that we ignore anxiety while getting on about our lives. We notice it. We do what can be done, realistically, to relieve it. However, we don't let the anxiety govern our lives. After all, when we see a yellow traffic light we have the choice to stop, to push through, to turn. The caution light doesn't control our driving; it informs us. Without it we would be in danger.

• Morita wrote that as neurotic sensitivity (shinkeishitsu) abounds so does our potential for greatness. He also wrote that if sensitive people try to become great they only sink into the trap of obsession; they become caught by their sensitivity. 86–4–49

Just as in Zen, when we try to achieve enlightenment by sitting in zazen meditation, just then it is impossible to achieve enlightenment.

PART V:

TALES OF CONSTRUCTIVE LIVING

In my earlier books, I included explanations after each story. Of course, those stories carried more of a teaching load than was contained in the appended explanations. Some readers merely fondled the commentary and moved on to the next story without kneading the tale fully.

Like Zen koan puzzles, these fairy tales for grownups may be best left to the individual to discover their interlocked meanings. So I have omitted commentary for many of the tales in this set. Which format do you prefer and why?

Aquarium

Lights shifting, shadows drifting, rippling, bubbles lifting, serene motion. Now turbulence, the flick of a tailfin, wriggling struggles.

Always motion. Always change. Always mediated by the wavy medium. Transition to transition. Ever flowing. Transforming. Reality.

The Good Ship Lollythink

Captain Happy launched his cruise ship, Lollythink, with a Hindu crew and a full complement of American passengers bound for the French port of Candide. The ship's activity program emphasized love, peace of mind, happiness, wealth, victory, laughter, and power. The ship's wheel was named Fortune, and each cabin was numbered "1." The good ship Lollythink was powered by twin Turbomagic engines rated in Megamindpower and costing Megabucks.

It was smooth sailing for everyone the first few days. Then a nasty wind blew up from the ice fields of the north. Despite the rhythmic chants of the engines and the positive attitudes of all on board, the waves rose to great heights. A reef of Reality loomed ahead.

Fearing the ship would crash and capsize, Captain Happy ordered all passengers to the lifeboats. The lifeboats were named It's New, Pop-psych, Fund'o'mental, Rx, and Dark Beauty, among others. Unfortunately, these lifeboats didn't hold water, so everybody ended up swimming for their lives in the churning sea. Some clung to the battered remains of the ship or the lifeboats; some drowned; some struck out on their own aiming for whatever looked like salvation. A few of the better swimmers made it to a sturdier vessel.

*   *   *

On the reefs of Reality the hulls of bliss philosophies lie shipwrecked. Only the Western sea of affluence and naïveté keeps fancy frigates afloat at all.

Constructive Living is put together simply, without grand sails, but it survives Reality's reefs and storms. It won't ferry you to paradise on earth, but it is sturdily built, and moves ahead at a reasonable pace. Oh, yes; it offers swimming lessons on board for crew and passengers.

Roshi

A. INDIRECTION

When ushered into the room, he found himself facing an old fellow with bright eyes beaming a welcome. He walked to within a pace of the old man, bowed his head to the floor and said, "Hello, kindly old grandfather."

The Roshi seemed to take offense at this mixture of familiarity and formality. He scowled and said, "What do you mean by that?"

"Ah, I see you are sometimes this, sometimes that," the younger man offered his reply.

Again, the Roshi's manner changed abruptly. "Well said; good." He relaxed, but his eyes were watching the newcomer like a cat watches a bird.

"Thank you. But the words are all borrowed."

"From whom?"

"Oh, from the walls, and from the lights, and from your eyes."

"Yes, they are fine teachers," responded the Roshi.

And from that time they were good friends, knowing each other in a way that some old friends never know each other.

B. COMMONPLACE

Another man entered the room and walked straight to the Roshi.

"About your book . . ." he began.

"My book is not so important. The experience it points to is important."

"You wrote here that . . ." the slim spectacled fellow continued unabashed. He began to read an extended quote from a translation of one of the Roshi's books.

The Roshi interrupted him. "Please put what you want to say in your own words, in everyday words. I don't understand the literary vocabulary of English very well. And you don't live your everyday life thinking in such terms."

Neither do I, nor do you.

C. UPROOTED

"What do you think about satori as ultimate identification with oneness?"

"I don't know anything about satori or oneness. I only know about things like how to pull up a weed by its roots and how to answer questions like yours."

D. OVERFLOWING

"Why don't you talk to that politician?"

"Because his cup is full—do you know that story?" (It is the well-known anecdote of the Zen master who kept pouring tea into his visitor's cup until it was overflowing. The visitor pointed out this fact, but the master kept pouring. Then he explained to his visitor that there was no more chance of putting more tea into an already full cup than of teaching something to a person whose mind is filled with preconceived ideas.)

"How do you know his cup is full?"

"Look at all those people filling it now."

E. NECESSITY

"The two masters made no special efforts to get together and talk. Why?"

"There are lots of people who need them. They don't need each other."

DAVID K. REYNOLDS

During a television interview:

"It is important to live well in this very moment. I think that performing-arts people, including talk-show hosts, thrive on the alertness to the here and now required by their work."

After a few minutes the director was signaling that time was running out.

"I give you a paragraph, but you have time to show only a word. I give you a paragraph because a word won't do. I have great sympathy for you. You are trying to do the impossible, in front of an audience."

G. EXPERIENCE

At a conference, the Roshi was challenged to debate a philosophical point.

"You invite me to play a game of academic ping pong with you. Why should I use simple hand gestures when I can speak in detail of what I've seen?"

The questioner, however, pressed him further to debate.

"I choose not to play, I said. Perhaps you, too will learn to distinguish the occasions when it is proper and improper to indulge in such academic pastimes."

H. RECOGNITION

"You are all my teachers and so are the garden and kitchen of my temple."

Two Rabbits

Once upon a muddled time a quick brown fox spotted two unsuspecting rabbits loping along a forest trail. The fox slipped up as close as possible, then leaped onto the trail just behind his prey. The rabbits, startled, veered off the trail in different directions, bounding as fast as they could.

The fox began chasing the one to the left. Then he thought he heard the other rabbit caught in some brambles off to the right. He took off after that rabbit. It struggled free of the brambles just in time to get a good lead on the fox. Meanwhile, the fox's sharp ears heard the first rabbit panting as it rested. Figuring that the rabbit on the left was tired from the initial chase, the fox returned to pursue that creature.

Back and forth the quick brown fox went, chasing one rabbit, then the other. The rabbits coughed and wheezed and feigned limps and falls to take the pressure off of each other.

Of course, the fox caught no rabbit that day.

Sometimes humans, too, become distracted from single-mindedness by more than one attractive purpose. There is only one purpose worthy of our attention in a given moment. First this, then that.

Tiger

There once was a young villager in India who was obsessed with the notion of killing a tiger with only his knife. The young man, Amar, was well on his way to becoming headman of the village. His wife was respectful and hardworking. Amar's reputation was without stain. He was honest, just, clever, and frugal—a good man by any villager's standards.

Amar was willing to put time and effort into achieving his ambitions within the village. No one doubted his ultimate success. But, then, no one knew of his odd desire to duel with a tiger in the wild.

The idea came to him one day as he sat with a group of men beneath a large banyan tree listening to a traveling storyteller. That afternoon the tales were about the gods of ancient days. Their superhuman bravery and powers made his puny efforts to rise to the headship of his small village seem petty and meaningless. If only he could duplicate the exploits of the gods, even once, Amar thought, he would be content to become a "mere" village chief. And what better way to challenge death than to fight with one of Nature's great killers, knife against claw.

Amar knew that he must not share his longing with anyone. If the villagers heard of his obsession they would laugh at his foolishness, they would lose some measure of respect for him. Even his wife, a sensible and conservative woman, would mildly suggest that he forget such a wild and unworthy idea. So Amar told no one, though the notion haunted him day and night.

At last, he felt he could wait no longer. He told his wife that he must visit a distant village on urgent business. Then he packed his traveling bag, strapped his knife to his waist, and headed for the trail into the jungle.

At the edge of the village he waved to his wife and called out, "If I am not back in two weeks you will know I am dead. This journey is dangerous, but I shall be careful. Good-bye." Then he turned and disappeared into the jungle.

In a little while Amar left the trail and entered the heart of jungle wilderness seeking his tiger. He was ready to fight at any moment. His hand gripped the handle of his knife. His eyes scanned the green world around him for signs of cat movement.

But all he saw that first day were some birds and a lone elephant off in the distance. How disappointing! Nevertheless, he decided not to return home until the duel was fought. He curled up in the fork of a tall tree and slept.

The next day he saw no tiger, and the next day, and the next. Once he thought he heard the barking cough of a big cat nearby, but he could find nothing. How discouraging, he thought. I have waited months for this fight, and now I cannot find an opponent. He continued his search.

On the fifth day, at last, he spotted his foe. It was a large tiger with golden fur as shiny as the sun's rays and stripes as black as the darkest night. It moved without noise, head swaying from side to side. It seemed to disappear and reappear as it padded among the jungle shadows. Amar stood bewitched by its powerful grace. He trembled. His knife seemed like a toy at his side.

Part of Amar wanted to run home to the safety of his village. A voice within made reasonable arguments for flight—after all, no one else knew of his quest. He wouldn't be shamed in the eyes of his fellow villagers for abandoning this uneven contest.

Another part of Amar warned him that running away this time would make running away from the next challenge easier. He would see huge tigers in every adversity. At all cost he must meet and overcome this obstacle to success.

DAVID K. REYNOLDS

Yet another part of Amar's mind was already trying to figure out a way to increase his odds of success if it came to a fight. A straightforward clash under ordinary conditions seemed hopeless. Amar decided to study the tiger before challenging it. Part of his mind shouted to begin the fight and get it over with; studying the situation was only an indirect way of avoiding and escaping from the challenge at hand. But Amar wanted to fight and win, if possible. To win he must first wait and watch. But he vowed that before the week was over he would be a victor or be dead.

His chance came a few days later. The cat was nervous, unaccustomed to being stalked by some other animal. But it was not too nervous to make a kill and eat its fill. It lay with forepaws propped up on the carcass of a small antelope. Gorged and drowsy it looked up at the bird plummeting from the sky. The bird was Amar dropping from a branch above with knife ready to plunge into the tiger's neck. The tiger twisted and rolled while Amer hung on with all his strength, jabbing again and again until the tiger bucked no more.

Then, scratched and bloody, Amar limped home. He told no one about how he came by his wounds, though most suspected it was a tiger's work. A few days later a villager found the remains of a dead tiger with Amar's knife beside it. Amar wouldn't talk about it.

Here's one model for handling a challenge. Pick an objective, accept your doubts and fears, scout the situation, and act.

Grass on the Slope

Her friend told her, "Keep on making chances for yourself, Honey. Maybe none of them will pay off. But you can't afford to wait for the world to create a chance for you. You don't want to do that to yourself. Even if a payoff comes you wouldn't deserve it, just sitting around waiting. Be a woman who sets up the odds in her favor again and again, if you need to. When you're that kind of woman the game is won already."

Now she sat on a grassy slope in late summer thinking. This grass doesn't care whether I'm divorced or successful or at peace. The grass knows only that winter will come. It stretches upward and anchors itself more deeply. As a hedge on survival it flicks its last wispy seeds into the flutterbreeze. It takes no particular notice of me as it goes single-mindedly about its seasonal business.

She felt comfortable there with her grassy companion. She was ignored, therefore free. Yet she wasn't alone.

We are constantly enveloped in the embrace of Reality. Our surrounding companions are numberless. Most of those companions go on about their way being what Reality dictates them to be. While setting up the odds to make Reality more like what we wish it to be, we must continue to recognize Reality for what it is.

Vacuum – Packed

Heddy reads old *TV Guide* magazines. She watches reruns of television quiz shows, sometimes shouting out the answers even before the questions are asked. She keeps videotapes of commercials for products she can no longer buy.

Sally was buried with an extra pair of her favorite shoes in the coffin.

Jerry types page after page of random-letter gibberish at the VA Neuropsychiatric Hospital Typing Clinic. He calls the ten thousand pages of single-spaced nonsense his "manuscript."

Franklyn pushes the floor button of the elevator exactly twice, then he pushes the close-door button exactly three times, then he presses against the bottom of the button panel with the palm of his right hand and waits expectantly for the door to close.

In the crossword puzzle of life the meanings may not be easily found. They are there, nevertheless.

Mango Mind

Once upon a time in ancient Iao Province, there was a disciple of a great master of Constructive Living. This disciple was given a seemingly insurmountable task by his master. He was ordered to write a great tale in which he would demonstrate with the clarity of the full moon reflected on Crystal Lake the elusive meaning of the master's esoteric teaching.

It must be said outright that this disciple was a rather insecure, indecisive fellow; bright, but somewhat lacking in confidence. He trembled at the very thought of beginning this monumental task. His pulse became rapid, his chest heaved, his palms beaded. He went to sit beneath the mango tree by the temple in hopes of finding some inspiration.

"If only I were a brave warrior who had fought in many fierce battles," he thought, "then the sheer force of my words would slice right to the heart of the teaching.

"If only I were a scholarly disputant, then the powerful logic of my arguments would extract the deep meaning of the teachings.

"If only I were a poet and singer of songs, then the pure sweetness of my words would lure out the meaning.

"But, alas, I am none of these. What am I to write about?"

As he sat there getting more and more anxious, he suddenly noticed a beautiful, ripe mango hanging within two feet of his nose. A mirror shattered in his mind. This was the most marvelous fruit in his experience!

He immediately set about writing a tale of an anxious, insecure disciple who spent so much of the time dreaming and wishing he were a warrior or a scholar or a poet that he nearly failed to notice something of exquisite beauty that existed right before his eyes. He rushed back to the temple with the mango and his tale.

When the master saw the mango in the disciple's hands he asked, "Where did you find that wondrous fruit?"

The disciple recounted the tale of warriors, scholars, poets, masters, disciples, and a mango. Thereupon the master cried, "That's it! Let's eat!"

As part of the certification training at the Health Center Pacific on Maui, the students are asked to write Constructive Living tales. This one was written by Dr. Brad Robinson.

By our daydreaming, anticipitory worrying, and dwelling on past failures we fail to discover and taste the ripest of Reality's fruits.

Professional Women

This is not a tale about women who are in business or professions like medicine or education. It is a tale about a country where being a woman had become a kind of profession. In that strange land there were specialized occupations called sex symbols, fashion models, pornography stars, actresses. Only females who worked in those fields were women. They defined what it was to be a woman. They dictated how a woman should talk and look and act. Other females tried to imitate them with varied degrees of success. But between Reality and ideals there is always a gap. The gap can be painful.

"Doctor, I need a man. I need someone to love me, someone I can love."

"What became of Arthur?"

"He left. He said he didn't want a long-term relationship. He said I wasn't what he was looking for. What's wrong with me? Why can't I hold onto a man? I try my best to be attractive . . ."

An hour later . . .

"Doctor, what am I looking for? None of the women I date seem right for me. Maybe I've set my sights too high. Maybe I'm looking for perfection in a woman. Will I ever find someone worth settling down with?"

"You sound as though you are tired of looking for the right woman."

"It's like going through a deck of cards, turning them over one by one. Some are clubs, some are diamonds, but they are all cards. They all have faults. I always go back to my videos and my fantasies. But the fantasies are satisfying only for a while. Then I'm driven back to my search for a real woman, a real relationship. What should I do? I try my best to find someone . . ."

In this unusual country the lady was not a real woman and the man sought a real woman who was really unreal. Confusing? Yes.

Of course, we don't have to adopt these images at all. We can work to be the best humans we can be, man or woman, alone or paired, in this very moment and circumstance.

DAVID K. REYNOLDS

Four Moon Tales

1. MOONCOMING

The moon finds a home in the lake, on the hood of a newly polished car, on her eyeglasses. It makes no special demands on those who provide it a place to rest. It comes and goes at the proper times, unhurried. The moon is always at home with its environment.

As clouds pass, the moon continues on its course. The sun rises, and the moon goes right on about its business. Its task doesn't require willpower, just obedience to its nature. Free? Constrained? Do such words have meaning?

2. MOONFALL

Tsuki worried that the moon would fall on her. Her fear began one night as she stood alone in her backyard enjoying the clear starry sky. She turned her attention to the full moon. As she stared at it the disk seemed to grow larger, as though it were falling toward the earth. She felt panic. Of course, her mind knew that the moon was safely orbiting as it always did. Nevertheless, she felt a clammy perspiration and a wave of vertigo as her eyes drifted back to the moon that appeared to be rushing toward her.

Tsuki turned her head away with an effort of will. She tried not to think about her strange fear. In the days that followed she worked to overcome her worry about such a ridiculous concern.

But the more she tried to banish the moon from her mind, the brighter it shone there.

She read poetry and essays in praise of the moon in order to get herself to love and appreciate it. But they merely called up visions of the expanding silver disk. She began to avoid going out at night, except when it was overcast, safe. But some nights, securely tucked in bed with shades pulled, she dreamed of a cyclops eye bearing down on her.

Words like "noon" and "mood" and even "harvest" and "full" and "crescent" bothered her; she tried to avoid using them, to avoid hearing or reading them. But all reminders of her fear couldn't be eliminated from her life. They appeared on the horizon like the rising you-know-what.

Tsuki's problem wasn't a misunderstanding about the moon. It was a misunderstanding about herself. She carried within herself the ability to sail the skies just as the moon does.

3. MOON MOODS

How can it be the same moon? Sometimes it is big, sometimes small; sometimes it is yellow, sometimes white; sometimes it is a crescent, sometimes round; sometimes high in the sky, sometimes low. How can it be the same moon?

Watch it. It is the same. It is different. It doesn't appear to move. But it moves. Observe.

"Mom," said little Kent, "the moon keeps changing. How can it be the same moon?"

"You keep changing, too," his mother replied. "How can you be the same Kent?"

"When I watch the moon, which is changing—the moon or me?"

4. MOONBURN

Jeff suffered from a rare disease, moonburn. Going out at night in the light of the moon caused his skin to glow and develop an uncomfortable rash. The disease was particularly distressing because Jeff suffered from insomnia at night, so that was the time he felt most active. During the day he took several naps, then he felt wide awake when night fell. But even the short walk from house to garage or from car to market caused him to pay the price of discomfort the next day. No amount of clothing or lotion seemed to protect him from the effects of the reflected rays of the moon.

Prescriptions for sleeping medication that would help him reverse his pattern and sleep at night seemed to have no effect. Jeff felt dejected and pessimistic about his chances to live any sort of healthy life. The more he tried to change his situation, the more upset he became when nothing seemed to work.

In despair he went to a writer of short stories and asked him to write a positive ending to the story of his life. Perhaps he could be made to fly off in a rocket to a distant inhabited planet with no rocky satellite circling it. Perhaps some miracle drug could be written into the story to introduce a cure for moonburn. Perhaps he could be turned into a miner or a mole or a permanent cave dweller of some sort.

But the problems of life stories are not always so easily solved as those in fiction . . . are they?

Junkies

In the mythical land of Dok there was a winged horse, Satori, upon which only a brave few had ever ridden. Those who rode upon this winged wonder appeared to be changed in some marvelous way. So it is no wonder that many desired to mount Satori.

How-to books concerned with tracking down the steed, gaining its confidence, and leaping astride its broad back were long sellers in the marketplace. And, of course, those who claimed to have ridden Satori could find an audience whenever they spoke.

Some of the fine citizens of Dok were what might be called "wing junkies." They bought every book about flying on Satori, took courses on mounting, attended lectures by famous riders, collected paintings and recordings of odd music that were supposed to be related to Satori.

These wing junkies had difficulty distinguishing what was genuine from what was fake. Anyone who used fashionable words and acted humble-superior could attract their attention and their money. In fact, for many of them, the goal of riding Satori had long ago given way to the goal of just thinking about riding it. The *idea* of the winged horse was so attractive that it was sufficient for these wing junkies.

There evolved a sort of informal club among the wing junkies of Dok. They saw each other at this academic lecture and at that bareback workshop. They exchanged clever words and techniques. They all considered themselves to be preparing for their big day with the heavenly steed, but, strangely, none of them ever actually rode it.

Over the years, a very few of the wing junkies dropped out of the chic movement. They gave up reading about the methods in order to try one of them—not for a weekend, but for a lifetime. Within a year or so, these dropouts discovered that what they thought they knew about galloping through the heavens was no more substantial than clouds. Their preparations took a new turn. Sticking to one method of riding wasn't nearly as much fun as tripping off to this "ashranch" and that communal corral. It took diligent effort and constant attention. Even then, some dropouts never found Satori, and some who found the horse never climbed aboard for their ride in the sky.

Even though witnessing the failure and difficulties around them, these dropouts knew in some mysterious way that they were closer to riding the stallion than when they had been wing junkies. They didn't understand how they knew this important truth, nor did they care. But the more they worked on the single method of riding, the closer they came to their goal.

Even fewer of these dropouts came to see the importance of cleaning stables and oiling saddles and practicing mounting leaps *whether they ever rode the winged steed or not.* Some folks saw these mundane dropouts and said that they were no different from the wing junkies. Both the stable sweepers and the wing junkies were "doing their thing." Neither would be likely to ride Satori. Both were satisfied with their preparations for riding.

But wing junkies and stable sweepers aren't the same at all. Stable sweepers no longer need to ride Satori. If the horse wanders through their stables they'll climb aboard, of course. But there is a great deal of satisfaction in keeping the stables shipshape.

The wing junkies, on the other hand, *need* Satori because their current life is unsatisfying. And they are likely to be forever frustrated, frantically flitting from equestrian tutor to cowboy guru.

In the land of Dok few fly the skies with Satori. Yet a few more have learned to walk the ground with winged feet.

The Magic Medallion

The adventurers sat hunched around a smoky fire in a hostile jungle. Each day brought them closer to their prize. Mountains, deserts, oceans, and now a jungle—but nothing would stop them. Natives emerged from the green curtain to advise them to go back. With one hand on their rifles they continued to eat from the tin plates propped on their knees.

They sought the magic medallion, source of great power. Power would bring them riches and lives of ease. So now they suffered this miserable, dangerous existence. The crumpled map in their leader's pocket traced an unclear path toward an uncertain destination. But they could feel the closeness of the medallion. It beckoned them to future fortune. Right now, the mosquitoes feasted and the fire ants stung, but if only they could gain the prize, all would be well.

After feats of daring and close escapes and long hours of boredom and weariness they stood before the Cave of the Magic Medallion. Cautiously they entered; who knew what final menace awaited them? Their flashlights crisscrossed back and forth on the walls of the shallow, manmade hole in the hillside.

The altar stood against the back wall. They approached it. Trapdoors? Deadfalls? Nothing. And on the altar, too, *nothing*.

Oh, no, they exclaimed, someone has beaten us to the medallion.

And then they read the inscription carved below the altar. It read:

"Foolish ones! Why do you seek magic power like little children lost in a fairy tale? Are you not adults? Did you not suffer and struggle to reach this place? You who succeeded in your quest have no need of magic powers. Go back and use the powers that are rightfully yours."

One of the adventurers returned home disappointed; he began to plan more expeditions, successful ones that would lead him to real treasure, not empty advice. A second member of the party picked up a few shiny pebbles near the altar. She hoped that they might have picked up some of the magical power of the medallion before it was stolen. An exhausted man ran screaming into the jungle and was never heard from again. But a handful of adventurers went home pondering the meaning of the inscription. What powers were rightfully theirs? Why should they have no need of wonderful magic? Had their expedition succeeded or not?

Running ◐

Once upon a timeless time, there lived on the edge of the Sahara Desert a slender striped antelope, Mahla. Mahla browsed from bush to bush, moving with a slight limp. As an adolescent she had been kicked and trampled by larger antelopes; her legs had never healed properly. Following that incident she had wandered off into the Sahara to die. After all, if others of her kind could treat her so cruelly she must not be worth much—at least so she thought at the time. But she had survived her time in the desert, and years had passed since then.

Mahla had discovered a way to keep from being trampled again. She attached herself to a big, powerful antelope whenever she joined a herd. She counted on that big one to protect her in case of a stampede. And, pretty much, the herd leaders cooperated in her plan.

There was a price Mahla had to pay, however, for her protection. She felt a need to keep in the good graces of her protector of the moment. She brought tasty clumps of grass and rubbed the tics away from her benefactor's side and tickled him with her horns. She felt frightened and defenseless when her protector wanted to be left alone or failed to show her affection and attention. To Mahla, it looked like her future depended on her male antelope and not upon herself.

The biggest price for Mahla was that her legs weren't getting stronger and her eyes weren't getting sharper. When an antelope depends upon itself, it keeps a sharp eye out for marauding lions and other dangers. It jumps at the slightest threat, so its legs grow stronger and faster. But Mahla felt safe (at least most of the time) in the shadow of her sturdy guardian. If she merely watched him . . .

On clear, sunny, safe days Mahla sometimes wandered away to join other foraging antelopes. Then she might criticize her guardian to the others, pointing out his weaknesses. When she saw him as weak, like herself, she felt less dependent and less fearful that he might leave her some day. Underneath this criticism was the recognition that she had forced herself into a subservient position to survive. She had to keep up a steady stream of services and a happy antelope face in order to stay in her protector's good graces.

Mahla wanted to stand on her own four legs, but she wanted security, too. She didn't want to put out much effort to change. After all, she was good at what she was doing already. And when the night was dark and packs of wild dogs howled nearby, it felt so reassuring to move to the sheltered side of her protector.

Fortunately, there is something about an antelope that refuses to allow it to be satisfied with anything less than the best it can be. Mahla began to take risks. Despite the danger involved she spent brief periods away from her shelter. And she wandered a bit further into the bush by herself. To be sure, when danger approached she immediately fled back toward security. But Mahla began testing the path of independence.

Among the low Mediterranean scrub bushes she encountered an old bushbuck. When Mahla began complaining about her protector the old bushbuck reminded her of all she had received from him. He suggested that she properly recognize her debts and keep on thanking her fellow antelopes for their services to her. When she spoke of her resentment about serving her guardian, the bushbuck advised her to serve him even more.

"But that's what got me into this mess," cried Mahla. "I'm a kind of guarded servant now, afraid to stop serving, afraid of being abandoned in a dangerous land."

"No, what got you where you are was your circumstance and

your cowardice and laziness. There's nothing wrong with service when it's really service and not some token payment for a hoped-for favor. You haven't been serving so much as repaying social loans.

"What I have in mind," the old bushbuck went on, "is real serving, without-expecting-anything-back serving. I'm talking about carrying a clump of grass to your friend, not your protector, then loping off to fend for yourself for awhile, giving both of you some space and room to grow."

"What you say sounds nice, I suppose. But it's scary, too," observed the young Mahla.

"It *is* scary. But do you want to walk with a limp all of your life? There's no longer anything wrong with your legs. You've adopted the habit of limping. You can run like the rest of the antelopes."

"I wonder," mused Mahla.

After much stumbling and many close calls, she did. In fact, she ran faster and more gracefully than most of the antelopes. With time, other antelopes began coming to Mahla for advice about how to run well. Imagine! Mahla teaching antelopes how to run!

Big Bucks

There once was a country where people measured the importance of things in terms of money. If a sporting event had big prize money it must be important, the people thought. If a quiz show gave away big money prizes it must be a fine show, people thought. If a man was rich he must be a terrific person, people thought. Expensive cars, expensive restaurants, expensive clothes all carried the aura of importance.

What a strange country! What foolish people!

The Perfectionist Prince

Once upon a time there was a prince who demanded 100 percent perfection from himself and from everyone around him, too. Needless to say, he spent a lot of time feeling disappointed because no one can live up to such high standards. He was disappointed in his father and mother (the king and queen); he was disappointed in the subjects of the land; and he was very, very disappointed in himself.

One morning he misplaced his favorite quill pen. He spent the whole morning searching for it. Then he pouted the rest of the day when it wasn't to be found. That was the sort of fellow he was. When life didn't go as smoothly as he expected, when Reality didn't turn out exactly as he wished, he was out of sorts.

It is no wonder that he spent a lot of time daydreaming about the more perfect times of the past—or so he remembered them. And he spent an equal amount of time hoping for a more satisfying future. Life just wasn't what it ought to be. And he was a prince, mind you.

There came a day when his body failed him. When his body worked properly he scarcely noticed it. His heart beat without his attention. His lungs pumped without any particular effort from his will. His hands and legs and tongue and eyes behaved in intricate ways to obey the general commands of his conscious mind. What operated automatically before demanded attention now. You can imagine the prince's upset.

For all of us there will come a stroke, or an accident, or the decrements of old age or some such limitation and pain. For the perfectionist prince, the change was devastating.

He lay on the bed in the royal clinic for weeks, hovering between death and life. That period of time was followed by more weeks of depression. When I visited him there he had pretty much recovered from the disease that had attacked him. He had this to say to me:

"I thought I had lost tomorrow," he smiled faintly. "I was so angry. Then I realized that I never owned tomorrow in the first place. When I started to get better, I wrote this poem. It's far from perfect, but it's realistic. Lying here for so long, I saw how far from Reality I had strayed."

He handed me a sheet of paper with this poem scrawled on it in scratchy, imperfect script:

Wandering Around in Nowhere with Now-here to Go

I thought I'd lost tomorrow
But it was never mine.
Future dreams that I adopted
helicopted to the ground
Leaving not a sign.

I thought I'd lost tomorrow
But it was never here.
Misty visions flowing, slowing
Failing to appear.

I thought I'd captured yesterday.
I wasn't very smart.
Within my mind I reached behind
And pressed time to my heart.

But yesterday was different
From what was in my thoughts.
The memories of ecstasies
Of coulds and shoulds and oughts.

DAVID K. REYNOLDS

While reveries distracted me
The days slipped by somehow.
I missed the chance to join the dance
Of living in the now.

I'm giving up tomorrow, forgetting yesterday
Oh, how can I do that?
Until I die I'll give a try
To being where I'm at.

Small Frog, No Pond

A small frog kept hopping from pond to pond looking for a place where he could feel at home. The ponds were scattered throughout the forest, and hopping over logs and rocks was exhausting work. It isn't surprising that the frog looked and felt worn out when he arrived at the next pond on his circuit.

You might wonder why he had so much trouble finding a place to settle down. Well, there were several reasons the frog himself knew about, and a few he didn't know about. He had friends at each pond, for one thing. He worried that finding a permanent home would prevent him from seeing friends in other ponds. Furthermore, he was a perfectionist, always looking for the *perfect* pond, which, of course, he would never find. He got bored easily, too. Finally, the other frogs looked forward to his visits because he brought news from other ponds. For the short while he visited each spot he was the center of attention—a daring little frog who braved the forest dangers for his periodic visits.

Perhaps, after all, it was his karma to be a traveler . . . whatever that means.

Nevertheless, a part of him wanted to find a home, a permanent home. Especially, as he passed from adolescence to young adulthood to middle age the discomforts of traveling and eating unfamiliar flies became more annoying.

He didn't complain. After all, this life was the one he had

chosen; no one had forced it upon him. But there were times during the solitary hops through the forest and times during the daytime sunning on foreign rocks when he felt an overwhelming urge to give up his jaunts. There might be just the right place for him in the next pond or the next. On the other hand, he really did like the attention that came with his travels.

Still, sometimes, just sometimes, his throat swelled and no sound came out, while a single teardrop formed in his bulging left eye. And he shivered as the cool night wind blew over his wet body.

Love Me Till It Hurts

Once there was June, the wife of a rich man, who doubted her husband's love. He treated her kindly and gave her everything she wanted. Still, she felt a nagging doubt about his affection for her.

"He is too perfect," she thought. "He is just playing out the role of 'good husband.' He has no real feelings for me. To him I am just playing out the role of 'good wife.'"

One night he came home late from a business meeting. June took advantage of the opportunity to quarrel with him over the late hour and some imagined mistress. He turned away, but she followed him, prodding, goading. In frustration he turned and slapped her.

In that moment June felt a curious mixture of relief and love and remorse and disappointment. He loved her, of that she was certain. After all, he had slapped her, hadn't he? But why did her smarting cheek signify love? Why did she feel guilt at provoking this display of emotion? Why was she disappointed in him? He behaved just as she had wished. She cried, fell into his arms, apologizing over and over. He apologized, too, genuinely regretting his display of temper. And, being a reason-dominated man, he wondered at what had come over the two of them to bring about this turn of events.

Curiously, her husband felt more distant from June, just as she felt a certain special closeness to him. The distance he felt was, in part, due to the awe he felt concerning her ability to draw out from him such ungentlemanly behavior. To exhibit such a loss of temper was, to say the least, embarrassing. Later, June interrogated herself. Would this one proof be enough? Would she need to provoke his temper again and again to reassure herself of his love? Could she find other ways of satisfying her need for certainty?

Dr. Kleinman swiveled his chair back toward his patient. "I am truly sorry we began our session late today, June. And I apologize for my outburst of temper. Let's meet again tomorrow at the same time, shall we?" He turned to the intercom, flicked a switch. "Miss Mead, would you please escort June back to her room? Thank you." Eyes dry now, June walked slowly from the office with bars on the windows.

The Mask

Yukari's mother gave her a small mask to play with as a child. Yukari would dress up in her mother's clothes and high-heeled shoes and pretend that she was a grownup woman. She would put on the mask and stick hairpins in her hair and parade in front of the mirror. She thought she looked just like a lady.

As she got older Yukari kept the small mask in her purse as a kind of good-luck charm. Once in a while, when no one was looking, she put on the mask and looked at herself in the mirror. Of course, her face was much larger than the domino now, and her face showed around its edges. Once, while she was looking at the mask in the mirror it felt stuck to her skin; she had trouble pulling it away from her face. But even when she took the mask off and looked in the mirror she sometimes imagined that her face still looked like its artificial covering.

The mask was made of a kind of cardboard. It couldn't last forever, no matter how carefully Yukari took care of it. At last it became so tattered that she had to throw it away. Then, little by little she forgot the old childish image of herself. She began to see Reality in the mirror.

When suffering people look in the mirror they see two images. The image they wish they were and the image that they are appear superimposed on each other. When the graduates of

Constructive Living look in the mirror, they see the reality of themselves.

Some people have taken the story to be about the neurotic desire to return to the presuffering self—the period before neurotic suffering began. But salvation doesn't lie in the past. We must begin by encountering the unmasked self in the present and reconstruct our faces by our actions.

Too Busy

The name of the country doesn't matter, and the exact year in the twenty-first century doesn't matter either. The government passed laws that increased the cost of food again. Tomiko was too busy cooking and shopping for the cheapest foods to protest the new laws. The school system was hurting her children by making them memorize day and night to pass difficult examinations. Tomiko was so busy helping the children with homework and keeping the house quiet so they could study that she never had time to protest the educational system, to talk to school officials or politicians who could change the educational system.

Tomiko's husband was a workaholic. He went to work early, came home late, and played golf every Sunday with his fellow workers. Tomiko had her hands full keeping his meals warm and his clothes ready for work. She never talked with him about changing his life-style. He was, after all, paying the bills with his income.

After a few years, her husband brought home a mistress to live in the house. Tomiko was quite busy preparing a room for the new guest in the house, learning what to cook for her and how to keep her pretty clothes ironed. Then the government set up a television camera in everyone's home so that officials could be sure that no one was doing anything wrong. Tomiko became more busy straightening up the rooms, making them clean and orderly for the television camera.

Then the school decided to do away with holidays and vacations so that the children could memorize Chinese, Russian, Arabic, and computer languages. Tomiko used all her spare time helping the children with the new homework assignments. There was talk of moving the children into school dormitories so they wouldn't be distracted from studying by a home life.

Television stations began showing only commercials and no other programs. So, of course, Tomiko began taking a course in understanding and appreciating television commercials.

She wondered why she was tired all the time. She thought she was doing what needed to be done. She was reacting to what reality brought her, wasn't she? But it seemed that the more she reacted in this way the more demands others made on her. The mistress wanted her clothes washed sooner. The husband wanted her to prepare lunches for some other men who worked in the office. The government wanted more cameras in the homes to observe everyone's actions. The school began to require mothers to come to school and attend classes with their children so they could help more efficiently with homework. Television stations broadcast a split screen so viewers could watch two commercials at once. Tomiko found less and less time for sleep as she rushed from one task to another.

She began to have dreams that her face was melting like hot wax while her arms and legs were sprouting strings that someone else was pulling.

"Where have I gone wrong?" she wondered. "I keep doing what is right in front of me to do, don't I?"

And then she made a fantastic discovery . . .

What discovery did Tomiko make? How do we determine what needs to be done? What is the proper relationship between what others say they want and what we should give them?

Constructive Living is not being busy all the time in the sense that Tomiko was busy. Where did Tomiko go wrong?

DAVID K. REYNOLDS

Specialization

Once upon a troubled time in a country between two oceans lived a people who forgot their ancestors. They focused so hard on staying young and healthy that they lost sight of the time-depth of human existence. Something had value only if it were instant. Instant food, instant enlightenment, instant entertainment, instant sex, instant education, instant marriage, and divorce. Faster than life, quicker than consideration, fleeting as a breath.

There was no time to develop ties with other humans on some informal level, so these people created specialist trades for instant solutions to human dilemmas. They created the profession of instant friend/advisor/supporter. For money, they could sit for a fifty-minute hour each week with someone who was expected to care for them. One problem that resulted from such an arrangement was that some people gave up all the other support in their lives in order to focus exclusively on this loving-for-money contractual relationship. They lived for this magical hour each week. Many found themselves disappointed and frustrated with such a narrowed life.

Another specialist trade developed in this odd country was that of professional backer/defender. Again, for money, people could find someone who would see that their rights weren't violated, that their grievances were settled to their advantage, that all disputes were worked out fairly. At least, that is how the system was supposed to work. And once more, there was great dissatisfaction with the actual working out of this way of handling human problems.

Similarly, in this country there were specialists who lent money (for a profit, of course), specialists who guaranteed spiritual salvation, specialists who took care of the beaten, the poor, the ill, the ugly, the ignorant. For every human difficulty there was some expert who (for a fee) could take care of it. For anyone with the means to afford the specialized services or anyone who had access to someone else's purse (including the government's purse), almost any problem could be handled almost instantly.

Interestingly, expert protectors didn't communicate well with expert curers or expert enforcers, expert educators didn't communicate well with expert lawmakers, expert friends didn't communicate well with expert moneylenders, and so forth. New specialists appeared who could communicate and mediate among other groups of specialists. No group had the time, after all, to learn the specialized ways of another group unless that was their specialty.

As the years passed there became family doctors and family lawyers and family bankers and family teachers and family therapists, as families tried to cover every base of potential human problems. As more years passed families, too, broke down into specialized roles. There was no need for the biological father to be the social father, for there to be a social father at all. Professional childkeepers arose.

Many of the everyday problems of living could be solved by these experts (and, often, relatively quickly). Nevertheless, there was something fundamentally unsatisfying about the fragmented, financial, fabricated, formal foolishness of it all. Was there no way to return to the human personal network of friends and acquaintances and family supporting one another in a variety of ways?

Well, not quickly. Certainly not instantly.

DAVID K. REYNOLDS

Danger Signs

Once upon an unsettled time there was a country in which women were considered ignorant and inferior until they became aroused and changed the attitudes of the whole populace. In the same country men were considered aggressive and dangerous until they became aroused and changed the attitudes of the whole populace.

Only after these changes were accomplished could children begin to grow up to be real adults.

Water World

Once upon a fragile time people lived on the surface of a huge body of water. They walked on a thin film that covered the water's great depths. Sometimes the surface tension weakened in spots and someone began to sink. Those around the sinking person risked breeching the surface tension in order to rescue him or her. It was the custom. Such self-sacrifice was necessary in that world. When the rescuers were in danger they, too, could expect help.

Sometimes, as the tear in the surface film spread, there were whole chains of people lending a hand to their fellows. In that risky world it was good to know that supporting hands were ready to help when needed.

Nearby, another group of people lived on a small island. They were proud that each of them walked by the individual's own strength with no help or support from others. In other ways they were a very bright people. Yet because of their pride they were confined to their island. And they knew a chilly loneliness that their water-borne cousins never felt.

One of the part-truths in American culture is the part-myth of the self-made individual. That notion has both stimulated us and limited us. The other side of that truth is that we are all dependent on others for our successes and for our moment-by-moment existence. The Naikan-inspired elements of Constructive Living assist us in recognizing this truth about mutual dependency.

The Lecture

He stood behind the podium small and bent and graying. The microphone was adjusted to its lowest height. A crystal pitcher of ice water and an upside-down glass sat on a tray at a small cloth-covered table at his side.

The audience sat silently, primly, expectantly. As he looked out he saw many men in their fifties and sixties with comfortable looks on their faces. There were fewer men in their thirties and forties, and these looked like hungry foxes in the dead of winter. There were even fewer women. Some of them were dressed like men. Everyone looked important. All were "professors" with a small "p." A very few were "Professors" with a "P" who mattered only a little more. All were representatives of the social and psychological sciences.

"I don't know what I can say to this august body that you don't already know," the little man began. "When the Council asked me to speak to you today, I debated with them and with myself about the appropriateness of this lecture. But, at last, I thought of something that you may not already have analyzed to your satisfaction. Today I'll demonstrate how to peel an orange."

With these words he moved to the side of the podium and drew from his bulging jacket pocket an orange and a paring knife. He began to cut a shallow circle around the top of the orange. There was a mild rustling in the audience. Was this some sort of introductory joke?

"I've spent thirty years mastering this technique." He turned his body slightly and spoke into the mike while intently watching his progress with the orange. "After the initial cut it is important to pry away the skin of the orange with the flat of the knife or you will nick the fruit."

He worked carefully for a couple of minutes, twice holding the orange up for all to see the progress. Finally, he placed on the table the peel held together at the bottom in one piece and pulled apart the unscarred orange into sections.

"This topic may not be worthy of your consideration. But words cannot do this small pilot study justice. The results of this project are unpublishable, but they are eminently edible." He proceeded to slip a section of the juicy fruit into his mouth. Many of those in the audience found themselves salivating.

"In your scholarly endeavors I implore you to incorporate research methods of the sort I have demonstrated to you today. I thank you."

Placing another section of the orange into his mouth and the remainder in his pocket, he sat down.

For a moment there was stunned silence. Then, from scattered places, applause.

Originally, this story was written for those social science academics whose research has become patterned meaninglessness. They may realize what has happened. But they continue to go through the motions of trivial discovery because to do so is easier and safer than changing, than enlivening their pursuits.

It turns out that some nonacademics find themselves in similar straits. Peeling oranges is more difficult than it appears, but the flavor of the result is indescribable.

DAVID K. REYNOLDS

Losing and Winning

Corinne's father died when she was only eight years old. As a grownup she couldn't remember much about him. Something he left her, though, was the fear that men would leave her. Corinne cried when she thought of losing someone.

Corinne tried all sorts of ways to keep men from leaving her. She learned to act sexually assertive and to talk tough in her attempts to please and emulate menfolk. She worked hard at warding off loss and rejection. And, pretty much, she succeeded. Corinne was a bright and beautiful lady. She revealed what talents she possessed and who she pretended to be to full advantage.

In the back of her mind, however, was a nagging question about who she really was.

Corinne had learned techniques to ward off the most dreaded possibility of life she could think of, but she hadn't learned to give herself away to someone who would give himself away to her. She had insured her measure of success with men, but found that success less than fully satisfying. She made sure that her interests were protected, but wondered at the cost.

Life brought Corinne opportunities now and then to sacrifice herself for someone else. Corinne saw these opportunities as dilemmas. Her friend was ill, but she couldn't afford to take time off from work to be with her. A boyfriend was willing to make a life commitment to her, but Corinne feared the entangling commitments of marriage. What if he discovered her true self (whatever that might be) after years of marriage and left her? It was all so difficult.

Corinne worked as an elementary school teacher. She found her work very satisfying. The headaches and long hours of working with barrio kids produced an odd delight in Corinne. School was the major part of Corinne's life in which her personal interests went unprotected. The salary raises and benefits were appreciated, but Corinne would have taught for free and worked on the side to earn money. There was something important about making sure that those kids got the best chance they could. She knew they needed her—her love and respect as well as her teaching ability. There was no problem with lack of confidence in this area of Corinne's life.

Why didn't Corinne figure out what you know already? Why didn't she transfer what she had learned as a teacher to her existence as a woman? In time, she did. She outgrew her childish self-protectiveness. She tried other ways of being with a gentle and patient man. When she discovered that being herself didn't scare him away she was so relieved that she began thinking some about *his* needs, *his* convenience, about protecting *him*. That put her on the track.

Just another happy ending-beginning.

Robin

Long ago, in the days before Skinner and Freud, lived Robin Robin. Robin was a young, "now-y" sort of bird who resisted the responsibilities of married life. She laid a couple of eggs then flew off to the local "hop" for entertainment, neglecting her duty to warm the eggs until they hatched.

At the hop Robin felt a nagging discomfort about what she had left undone, so she flew back to her nest and deposited a couple of extra eggs, just in case the first two didn't hatch on their own. Then back she flew to the hop.

But again, Robin worried about the fate of her eggs. Would some weasel get to them while she was gone? Back she went to the nest to lay more insurance eggs. But sitting there all day didn't appeal to her. She was born to fly (and hop). Soon she was back at the festivities.

Robin continued her flights back and forth between her nest and the hop until the pile of eggs grew so large that the newly laid eggs fell off the mound, out of the nest, and crashed upon the ground below. Poor Robin! She wept and beaked her breast until it became inflamed. And you know the rest.

When: 1) you know something needs doing; and 2) you don't do it; then 3) knowing you didn't do it/aren't doing it interferes with doing the next task; and 4) makes you feel uncomfortable.

Preparations

For three years in a row the winter snow had fallen heavily. Roofs caved in, stores of food ran out, the villagers huddled together for warmth around the few remaining fires. Those were dark, cold, miserable days.

In time spring came, late but seemingly more luxuriant because of the delay, and the villagers emerged from their lairs stretching and blinking and hoping again. They ate new green shoots and washed their sooty clothes and marveled at the beauty of dogtooth violets. And they forgot about winter.

Some of the older, wiser villagers warned the others that winter would come again. They must prepare for it just as the plants and beasts do. But winter was past and who knew when it would return? Most of the villagers simply enjoyed the good, warm times and turned away from thoughts of what might happen in some distant future time.

They didn't change their behavior. They didn't change their attitude. They stored away body fat and good memories. Until the next winter.

Some of my students are like the villagers. They come to me (or go to a psychiatrist or minister or other therapist) when winter storms of feeling blast them. When the weather clears they loll in the sunshine, making no preparations for future storms.

Such people are still feeling-centered. When they are feeling fine they see no need for change. When they are feeling terrible they desire most fervently to change something, anything, to escape from their misery.

There are ways to ready ourselves so that winter may be unpleasant but not tragic. No one escapes an occasional winter storm. But by becoming action-centered rather than feeling-centered we can keep reasonably warm during the most chilling days. We cannot wait until winter to begin working on ourselves, however, if we wish to make changes most effectively in our lives. Preparation for winter must begin in the spring.

DAVID K. REYNOLDS

Smarts

Once upon a wishful time pocket-sized dragons roamed the land. They attacked humans at will. They attacked anything in sight. Their bites rarely killed, but they were painful and took time to heal. People walked about with scars.

A philosopher arose who claimed that getting to know the dragons would cause them to cease their attacks. He and his followers made great efforts to understand and communicate with the miniature dragons. As a result, they suffered many bites, but they gathered much information about the dragons' habits.

Unfortunately, the philosopher was wrong. Knowing a lot about dragons didn't stop them from attacking. The people felt despair. Some tried to appease the dragons with every kind of personal gift and sacrifice imaginable. But giving in to the dragons seemed to be ineffective, also. In fact, sacrificing their material possessions to try to keep the dragons at bay proved more costly than enduring the occasional bite. What could they do? The people were at a loss.

All sorts of methods proved unworkable. Heavy armor restricted the wearer's movements. Flight to the mountains and beaches demonstrated only that dragons existed in those places, too. Prayers didn't destroy the dragon demons.

In time, the people learned to live with occasional pain. They avoided areas heavily infested with dragons. They kept their eyes open to avoid stepping into the path of a dragon. But they learned to go about their daily lives wearing a bandage here and there. Often, they were so involved in their work or play that they forgot about the pain, the bandages, the dragons. Such was the nature of the country.

Psychological insight doesn't erase pain or prevent its reoccurrence. It may help us spot potential trouble areas. Though we avoid what is avoidable, we cannot escape from hurt altogether. We live alongside it; we live within it; we live it. And the way we live in spite of our pain is a measure of our character.

I am told that in the dragon-infested country introduced above some people actually befriended and even married particularly large dragons. And, despite differences in their temperaments, they seem to have gotten along together pretty well.

New Age

Marge was born in a time and place where the world made allowances. Folks knew your family; they knew you from the time you were first brought to church all wrapped up in a flannel blanket. The air was moist with all sorts of understanding that took years to develop and lots of personal investment to maintain.

When Marge moved to the dry atmosphere of the big city she expected the world to be as it was back home. But she found a more arid, concrete and petroleum environment. As the years passed she grew to love the excitement and convenience of the city. The city created needs in her that would prevent Marge from ever returning to old times and places except for brief, nostalgic visits.

What Marge never got used to was the impersonal attitude of machines. Machines don't care who you are. They don't take into consideration your intent or your reputation. They don't know if you have a good heart. Electrical appliances short out and kill people indiscriminantly. Cars run you over whether you are coming from a baptism or a brothel. Phone answering machines respond to the button you actually push, not to some estimate of what it figured you really wanted to do. Machines just do their thing. They break down without any concern for the convenience of humans. For Marge, it was all too darn thoughtless—like the difference between the touch of a formica surface and that of human skin.

Some people who lived around machines in the city for a long time seemed to adopt a similar mechanical attitude toward life. They dried out. They went about their jobs and home lives on automatic. They responded when their buttons were pushed with no real concern about how their reactions would affect others. They were predictable, reasonably efficient for human machines, troublesome only when provoked.

Marge never could get used to the impersonality of machines and machine-people. Yet she would never choose to retreat to the warm rural wetness of her childhood world with its physical inconvenience and restrictions. What could she do?

Marge was a clever woman, and a sensible one. She built a little greenhouse right in the middle of the city. She surrounded herself with other folks who had the same background as she. She developed a network of friends and neighbors who looked after one another in traditional ways while enjoying the stimulation of city life. She included a few friends who were good with machines, accepted their minor repairs and instructions, and endured their scolding when she misused and broke her microwave oven and her video recorder and her stereo phonograph. In return she offered a listening ear, sound advice, home-baked pastries, sick-bed visits, errands, and other human services.

Marge couldn't make machines into humans, but she could help keep some humans from becoming machines.

DAVID K. REYNOLDS

PART VI:

POSTSCRIPT

Psychotherapy: East and West

I. IN THE WEST

One can see a pattern in the development of psychotherapy in the West. Phillips (1985), for example, sees a progression of major contributions beginning with Freud, followed by Rogers, and then the behavior therapists. In this trend I see an expansion of the conceptual locus of the problem of neurosis. Freud saw neurosis as an intrapsychic problem, handled by intrapsychic manipulations. Rogers saw neurosis as growing from reflections of others and reactions to others. Cure was sought through more constructive dyadic interactions in the therapy setting. The behaviorists see neurosis as developing from the situational pressures and behavior history of the individual. Cure comes by way of changed behaviors and changed environmental constraints.

Increasingly, the present ongoing environment has been introduced in a clear, yet broad, fashion as a major contributor to neurosis. Yet, there is another step that needs to be taken. All these Western therapies view neurotic suffering as something "added" to the individual, something that can be removed by proper manipulations. None has yet properly placed the individual within the environment, *as part of the environment*. This step is the natural culmination of the previous broadening. The impetus for this newest progression comes from the East. By incorporating some notions from Morita therapy and Naikan therapy we move to a truly naturalistic perspective on neurosis and cure.

Incorporating the notion of environment into our notions of self, neurosis, and cure, new possibilities are opened for theorists and clinicians. Neurosis is no longer seen as a malignant condition imposed on the client by the psyche or by social influences or by other external environmental factors. Neurosis is the experience of suffering unnecessarily that occurs in certain situations. That suffering is as natural a part of the environment as my concept of "myself" or the cough that accompanies an irritation of the throat.

The goal of therapy, then, shifts away from trying to remove "symptoms," which have been defined as unnatural and capable of eradication, and shifts toward teaching a lifeway that allows more fluid and constructive movement as part of the environment. The clients no longer see themselves as struggling with their anxieties (putting their own stream of awareness in conflict with itself), for example, but as fitting themselves to the Reality that they are part of and doing what they can to make a contribution to that Reality.

Thus, psychotherapy is not remedial or surgical, but expanding and incorporating in its thrust. "Symptoms" aren't removed; they are outgrown, encompassed, accepted-to-death.

Lakin Phillips also makes the point that Western therapy seems to monopolize the Western patient's help-seeking, thus limiting the seeking of or maintaining other natural areas of support. I think he is right. Many of my students want to meet often, depend on me and not on themselves or others, pay money for support and advice. In Japan and in the United States they seem to want a sort of division of labor—they want to expose their weakness and failures and anxieties in the therapy setting and maintain an aura of competence in their other social relations. They seek a sort of institutionalized "time out." They seem uncomfortable talking about their successes and accomplishments in therapy—in fact, as noted earlier, one young lady actually makes up excuses not for her failures but for her successes, as though they had no part in the therapy hour.

It is time to give serious thought to what psychotherapy is about and what it ought to be about.

DAVID K. REYNOLDS

Shared by many Eastern approaches to mental health is the admonition to view Reality as it really is, not the way you expect it to be or the way you have been taught it should be. Learning a non-Western lifeway, through experience, prepares us to view our own lifeway through different eyes.

Looked at from another perspective, our vaunted Western "team approach" to psychotherapeutic treatment seems less concerned with curing anyone and more concerned with helping professionals untangle their roles and protect their specialty turf. Like most of our therapeutic structures and practices, this approach is set up for the convenience, protection, and comfort of the staff and not for the support of patients. Frankly, no one knows very much about how to go about helping suffering humans, so it's not too surprising that all this self-serving social undergrowth springs up.

I read about the pinpoint accuracy of psychopharmacology, but what I actually see in the world is, "let's try this medication and see what happens—now let's try that medication and see what happens." We train professionals to work in our outpatient clinics as though they will be seeing clients for long periods of time, yet E. Lakin Phillips has found across a variety of types of outpatient clinics in several cultures that we see the modal number of clients only once, the next highest group only twice, and so on in a predictable curve. That's reality. We need to be training our young psychotherapists to gain skills at one-shot therapy, for that is what they are likely to encounter most often. What we teach in our professional schools as fact is really more like some normative fiction—the way someone thinks therapy ought to be. But again, no one knows much about what therapy ought to be. Meanwhile, those in power have to appear as though they did. Some of them probably have convinced themselves that they know more about psychotherapy than they do. They believe the fictions and fantasies they have been taught.

I am not saying that there is no tangling social undergrowth in medical or educational settings in Japan. The medical profession there has borrowed a lot of our American medical ways just as some Japanese have borrowed rock music and Kentucky Fried

Chicken and coin laundries. But the undergrowth is somewhat more visible because it is different from our own.

And the medical establishment in Japan is no more skillful at teaching the therapeutic lifeway of Constructive Living in order to alleviate suffering than are its American colleagues with Western methods. The lifeway we teach remains "clean" because it is Reality-based. One way to teach psychotherapy in our professional schools would start by turning naive students loose in therapy settings. Let them compare what they see with what their teachers see, let them observe without the prejudice that what their teachers see in these same settings is a clearer or more accurate view of what is going on. Just compare. Let us look once more at Reality.

II. IN THE EAST

Another sort of broadening has taken place in Morita therapy, one of the methods underlying Constructive Living. In Morita's day, the focus was on work, particularly physical labor in the service of others, as the basic element of a Constructive Life. This focus has been broadened in modern times to encompass any purposeful activity: not only work but sports, hobbies, travel, and other recreational pursuits. In similar fashion, the narrow application of Morita therapy to a diagnostic category of neurosis called "shinkeishitsu" has given way to the application of the method to other types of neuroses, and to non-neurotic people, as well. Recent applications to the everyday living aspects of therapists and terminally and chronically ill patients show this broadening trend.

I suspect that the increasing need for people to learn the Constructive Living lifeway is related to the increased prosperity of our age. As our societies prosper we have more to protect, more potentially to lose. We become increasingly concerned with health and with dying. We want to hold on to and enjoy the fruits of our material possessions as long as possible. We see that social success brings obvious material and nonmaterial rewards, so we covet success and fear failure. We see that rationality and cognition have solved many technological problems and hope to turn the same light of intellectual problem-solving on our private lives.

DAVID K. REYNOLDS

Furthermore, as we see greater and greater improvements in the ease of our everyday lives, we hope for and demand ever fancier devices and services. Our ideals and dreams sail ever beyond the rapid technological progress.

The trends to be self-protective, to focus on health concerns, to strive for social success and dread failure, to try to solve life problems with an intellectual approach, and to have perfectionistic, idealistic tendencies, were characteristic of the "shinkeishitsu" neurotics of Morita's day. This therapy was developed for just the sort of people we have become. It isn't surprising, then, to see the expansion of the techniques and applications to an ever-widening circle of students of this method.

References

Blyth, R. H. *Zen and Zen Classics,* ed. Frederick Franck. New York: Vintage, 1978.

Dogen and Kosho Uchiyama. *Refining Your Life,* trans. Thomas Wright. New York: Weatherhill, 1983.

Fujita, Chihiro. *Morita Therapy.* New York, Tokyo: Igaku-Shoin, 1986.

Haskel, Peter. *Bankei Zen.* New York: Grove Press, 1984.

Iwai, Hiroshi, and David K. Reynolds. "Morita therapy: the views from the West." *American Journal of Psychiatry,* 126(7), 1031–1036, 1970.

Kobusa, S. C., et al. "Hardiness and health: a prospective study." *Journal of Personality and Social Psychology,* 42, 168–177, 1981.

Kondo, Akihisa. "Morita therapy: a Japanese therapy for neurosis." *American Journal of Psychoanalysis,* 13, 31–37, 1953.

Kopp, Sheldon. *If You Meet the Buddha on the Road, Kill Him!* New York: Bantam, 1972.

Kora, Takehisa. "Morita therapy." *International Journal of Psychiatry,* 1(4), 611–640, 1965.

——— and Kenshiro Ohara. "Morita therapy." *Psychology Today,* 6(10), 63–68, 1973.

Miura, Momoshige, and Shin-ichi Usa. "Morita therapy." *Psychologia,* 13(1), 18–34, 1970.

Miyamoto, Musashi. *A Book of Five Rings,* trans. Victor Harris. Woodstock, N.Y.: Overlook, 1974.

Morita, Shoma. *Seishin Ryoho Kogi.* Tokyo: Hakuyosha, 1983.

Ohara, Kenshiro, and David K. Reynolds. "Changing methods in Morita psychotherapy." *International Journal of Social Psychiatry,* 14(4), 305–310, 1968.

Reynolds, David K. *Morita Psychotherapy* (English, Japanese, and Spanish editions). Berkeley: University of California Press, 1976.
———. "Naikan therapy—an experiential view." *International Journal of Social Psychiatry*, 23(4), 252–264, 1977.
———. *The Quiet Therapies*. Honolulu: University of Hawaii Press, 1980.
———. "Morita Psychotherapy." In *Handbook of Innovative Psychotherapies*, ed. R. Corsini. New York: Wiley, 1981.
———. "Naikan Therapy." In *Handbook of Innovative Psychotherapies*, ed. R. Corsini. New York: Wiley, 1981.
———. *Naikan Psychotherapy: Meditation for Self Development*. Chicago: University of Chicago Press, 1983.
———. *Constructive Living*. Honolulu: University of Hawaii Press, 1984.
———. *Playing Ball on Running Water*. New York: Morrow, 1984.
———. *Even in Summer the Ice Doesn't Melt*. New York: Morrow, 1986.
———. *Water Bears No Scars*. New York: Morrow, 1987.
——— and Norman L. Farberow. *Suicide: Inside and Out*. Berkeley: University of California Press, 1976.
——— and C. W. Kiefer. "Cultural adaptability as an attribute of therapies: the case of Morita psychotherapy." *Culture, Medicine, and Psychiatry*, 1, 395–412, 1977.
Shah, Idries. *The Sufis*. New York: Doubleday Anchor, 1964.
———. *Caravan of Dreams*. Baltimore: Penguin, 1968.
———. *Thinkers of the East*. Baltimore: Penguin, 1971.
Suzuki, Tomonori, and Ryu Suzuki. "Morita therapy." In *Psychosomatic Medicine*, ed. Eric D. Wittkower and Hector Warnes. New York: Harper & Row, 1977.
———. "The effectiveness of in-patient Morita therapy." *Psychiatric Quarterly*, 53(3), 201–213, 1981.
Trungpa, Chogyam. *Glimpses of Abhidharma*. Boulder, Colorado: Prajna Press, 1975.
———. "An Approach to Meditation." In *The Meeting of the Ways*, ed. John Welwood. New York: Schocken, 1979.
———. "A Dialogue with Psychotherapists." In *The Meeting of the Ways*, ed. John Welwood. New York: Schocken, 1979.
Usa, Genyu, and Shin-ichi Usa. "A case of a nun who suffered from visionary obsessions of snakes, treated by Morita therapy." *Psychologia*, 1, 226–228, 1958.
Welwood, John, ed. *The Meeting of the Ways*. New York: Schocken, 1979.
Wilber, Ken. *No Boundary*. Boulder, Colorado: Shambala, 1981.
Yamamoto, Tsunetomo. *Hagakure*, trans. William Scott Wilson. New York: Avon, 1981.

For more information on Morita and Constructive Living write or call:

ToDo Institute
P.O. Box 17868
Los Angeles, CA 90017-0868
(213) 389-6155

Center for Constructive Living
P.O. Box 460696
San Francisco, CA 94146-0696
(415) 641-4841

Health Center Pacific
P.O. Box 1081
Wailuku, HI 96793
(808) 242-9711

Constructive Living Institute
P.O. Box 4116
Kingston, NY 12401
(914) 331-1624

About the Author

David K. Reynolds, Ph.D., has been on the faculty of UCLA, the University of Southern California School of Medicine, and the University of Houston. He is the director of the ToDo Institute in Los Angeles. He travels among Constructive Living centers in Los Angeles, Hawaii, Tokyo, and New York, lecturing, training, and conducting a small private practice in English and in Japanese.

Dr. Reynolds is the author of more than fifteen books published in the United States and Japan. Recent titles include *Water Bears No Scars, Even in Summer the Ice Doesn't Melt, Playing Ball on Running Water, Constructive Living, Naikan Psychotherapy,* and *The Quiet Therapies.*

Other books by David K. Reynolds in the Quill series:

Playing Ball on Running Water

An exploration of the Morita lifeway, which shows how to overcome our neuroses and choreograph life as precisely and aesthetically as the Japanese tea ceremony.

Even in Summer the Ice Doesn't Melt

A deeper examination of Morita psychotherapy and an introduction to another Japanese philosophy, Naikan, which is based on recognizing our debts to the people and things around us.

Water Bears No Scars

A mix of essays, exercises, and fables to illustrate how every action—even one as simple as washing the dishes or dialing the telephone—can become an opportunity for character development and growth.